UNDERSTANDING UNITED STATES GOVERNMENT GROWTH

An Empirical Analysis of the Postwar Era

William D. Berry
and
David Lowery

PRAEGER

New York
Westport, Connecticut
London

Library of Congress Cataloging-in-Publication Data

Berry, William Dale.
  Understanding United States government growth.

  Bibliography: p.
  Includes index.
    1. Finance, Public—United States—1933–
—Econometric models. 2. Government spending policy—
United States—Econometric models. 3. United States—
Politics and government—1945–   —Econometric
models. I. Lowery, David. II. Title.
HJ257.2.B47 1987   336.73   87-11818
ISBN 0-275-92509-9 (alk. paper)

Library of Congress Catalog Card Number: 87-11818
ISBN: 0-275-92509-9

First published in 1987

Praeger Publishers, One Madison Avenue, New York, NY 10010
A division of Greenwood Press, Inc.

Printed in the United States of America

The paper used in this book complies with the Permanent
Paper Standard issued by the National Information Standards
Organization (Z39.43-1984).

10 9 8 7 6 5 4 3 2 1

For Caryl, David, Fran, and Katie

CONTENTS

LIST OF TABLES

LIST OF FIGURES

PREFACE

The research program of which this book is a major part began, as many research programs do, with a student's question. When one of us was presenting some of the many explanations of the growth of the public sector in the postwar period to a class on public budgeting, a student asked if we had identified which one of these models was best able to account for government growth. Although it was a simple question, we had no simple answer. There were an inordinately large number of competing hypotheses in the relevant theoretical literature. And nearly all these hypotheses had received at least some empirical support. Indeed, in our review of literature, the most accurate statement on the state of knowledge about government growth was Larkey, Stolp, and Winer's (1981, p. 202) comment that they were "impressed with how much has been written and how little is known about why government grows."

We take a step toward resolving this confusion with the work presented in this book. Quite simply, we confront a number of the extant accounts of public sector expansion with data, using better measures of the size of government than commonly found in the literature. Finding that most of the existing explanations do not survive that encounter, we develop and test two alternative theories of government growth.

These two theories — the *responsive* and *excessive* government interpretations — were chosen so that we could use our empirical analysis to comment on the important normative and policy issues that give this topic such immediacy. The public sector is under attack to a degree never experienced since the advent of "big government" in the 1930s. Such varied but related events as Proposition 13, "Reaganomics," and "Gramm-Rudman-Hollings" represent a profound set of challenges to an expanding public sector. And importantly, there is at least an implicit "theory" of government growth behind the new antigovernment ideology, a theory asserting that the causes of public sector expansion lie within the public sector. With the design of our responsive and excessive government models of public sector size, we attempt to pit that implicit · theory against an older, alternative account that views government expansion as an outgrowth of changing citizen preferences and socioeconomic needs. Using the tools of econometric analysis, we test the two models using data on U.S. government size over the postwar era, 1948–1982.

Empirical analysis of this type obviously will not provide a definitive account of the causes of public sector expansion. As will be seen in this book, limitations of theory and data prevent us from identifying an answer of the kind our student was hoping for when he asked the question that sparked our interest in the topic. And even more important, empirical results speak only indirectly to the many underlying normative concerns associated with the issue of big government. Questions of freedom, liberty, and even efficiency are difficult to address with the kinds of professional tools we use in this book. Still, we will see that while inherently less than definitive, the empirical findings have a number of important implications for many of these normative issues.

Most of the data used in the empirical analyses presented in the book are from CITIBASE, a time-series data base maintained by the Economics Department of Citibank and made available to us through the University of Kentucky Center for Applied Economic Research. We thank them for making this incredibly rich "public good" available to us, but neither Citibank nor the Center for Applied Economic Research bears any responsibility for the analyses or interpretations presented here.

I

GOVERNMENT GROWTH: MEASUREMENT, CONSEQUENCES, AND CAUSES

1

THE PROBLEM OF
GOVERNMENT GROWTH

INTRODUCTION

President Reagan expressed the underlying theme of his new administration when, in his 1981 inaugural address, he declared, "it is time to check and reverse the growth of government" (Hartman 1982, p. 266). Such concern for the dangers of excessive government is hardly new to the rhetoric of U.S. politics, but the Reagan administration turned with unusual zeal to the task of cutting the domestic budget and scaling back the regulatory burden of the public sector (Palmer and Sawhill 1982; 1984). Unlike past administrations, the rhetoric of scaling back government activity led to action. As Palmer and Sawhill (1984, p. 2) note, "The Reagan administration, more than most others, has had a clear vision of what it was trying to accomplish. Its continuing objective . . . [has] been to reduce the size and influence of government."

This "clear vision" arises from the confluence of traditional libertarian perspectives on the relationship between government and the market and the newer but rapidly growing "public choice" literature on the operation of government and politics. The former provides the critical standards for evaluating the size of government but is woefully lacking in positivist statements about the operation and dynamics of the public sector (Stigler 1982, pp. 136–45). Consequently, the traditional libertarian philosophy tells us much more about what government should not do than about what it actually does. In contrast, public choice theory (Buchanan 1975; Mueller 1979) applies the analytical tools used

3

by traditional libertarians in the analysis of market transactions to the processes of government and politics. The new *conservative critique* of excessive government is derived from this dynamic mix.

The conservative critique contains views about the consequences of big government, the causes of government growth, and the solution to the perceived problem. The major consequence is a loss of both freedom and efficiency. President Reagan alluded to the loss of efficiency in his inaugural address when he promised to remove "the roadblocks that have slowed our economy and reduced productivity" (Nathan 1983, p. 161). He also capsulized the conservative critique's position on what is responsible for government expansion when he warned, "Government is not the solution to our problems; government is the problem" (Nathan 1983, p. 159). Thus the public sector has not grown in response to objective needs of the nation, but instead in response to the selfish needs of government itself. Moreover, if the causes of excessive government expansion arise from within government, then major institutional reforms will be needed to bring the size of government within reasonable limits — solutions such as tax limitations, "fiscal caps," or constitutional balanced budget restrictions (Meltsner 1982; Rabushka 1982).

How valid is the conservative critique? This is a question we attempt to evaluate, at least partially, in this book. Specifically, we examine the determinants of size of government in the United States in the post–World War II era. Although our attention is directly focused on the causes of public sector growth, the findings have important implications for the other components of the conservative critique of big government. For instance, the solutions to big government called for in the conservative critique may not be adivsable if the critique's view of the causes of government expansion proves to be incorrect.

In the remainder of this chapter, the conservative critique of government growth is reviewed in greater detail to lay the foundation for our examination of the determinants of public sector size in the United States. Specifically, we assess the consequences and causes of big government and the solutions proposed to control its growth.

THE CONSEQUENCES OF BIG GOVERNMENT

Big government has been criticized for many reasons, including the costs of higher taxes and the burdens of extensive regulation and stifling interactions with heavy-handed bureaucrats. But from the perspective of the conservative critique, these many criticisms add up to a twofold indictment of a large public sector.

First, public production of goods and services is viewed as inherently less efficient than private production. Not surprisingly, this view is founded on the rock of Adam Smith. As Milton and Rose Friedman (1980, pp. 13–14) have suggested:

> Adam Smith's flash of genius was his recognition that the prices that emerge from voluntary transactions between buyers and sellers — for short, the free market — could coordinate the activity of millions of people, each seeking his own interest, in such a way as to make everyone better off.... Prices perform three functions in organizing economic activity: first, they transmit information; second, they provide an incentive to adopt those methods of production that are least costly and thereby use available resources for the most highly valued purposes; third, they determine who gets how much of the product — the distribution of income.

In this prototypical interpretation of Smith's vision, the free market, through the price mechanism, encourages efficient use of resources through the unforgiving force of competition and distributes income without government intervention on the basis of relative abilities to produce what the market values.

In contrast, the public sector — according to the conservative critique — is virtually by definition an inferior vehicle for pursuing economic activity. Lacking self-directing organization through the price system, the public sector must be organized by hierarchical direction. Lacking the goad of competition, government has no incentive to eliminate the inefficient or reward the efficient. And lacking a neutral means of distributing income, government must act to distribute income on the basis of political criteria.

Accordingly, expansion of the public sector into activities formerly provided through the free market entails an efficiency loss (Friedman and Friedman 1980; Brennan and Pincus 1983; Lindsey and Norman 1977; Friedman 1978, pp. 52–81; Aranson and Ordeshook 1981). Such beliefs surely motivated the "supply-side" tax program of the Reagan administration (Lekachman 1982; Rousseas 1982; Gilder 1981; Wanniski 1979) but have been part of the conservative critique for far longer.

The second consequence of excessive-sized government is a loss of freedom. Friedman (1962) has long argued that economic freedom is in and of itself an integral part of total freedom (see also Buchanan 1975). As a separate source of power in a society, the market constitutes a realm of activity outside the potentially tyrannical entity of government. And importantly, the exercise of economic power in the market sector, with its emphasis on voluntary exchange and competition, is definitionally the antithesis of tyranny. Moreover, the mere existence of private economic power serves as an important counterbalance to the exercise of political power, thereby serving to guarantee political freedom as well. A large public sector, then, necessarily reduces the scope of total freedom by limiting economic freedom and by reducing the effectiveness of the countervailing force of the market on potentially tyrannical political power.

Not surprisingly, these various elements of the conservative critique of the consequences of big government have not gone uncontested. Its view of both the freedom and efficiency advantages of limited government has drawn a host of challenges. But, the unreconstructed "Smithian" perspective on efficiency has probably been challenged in the most direct manner.

First, a number of analysts have attacked the presumed efficiency advantages of the market by rejecting the critique's assumption that the actual organization and operation of private production conforms to the analytical ideal of Smith's model. For instance, the market failure literature flowing from Pigou's (1946) observation that total social and individual costs (and benefits) of production often diverge suggests that prices are not always the ideal coordinating device (see also Burkhead and Miner 1971, pp. 97–144). And Galbraith's (1958; 1969) introduction of nonmarket based power into the analysis of private sector decision making even more fundamentally undercuts the presumed efficiency advantage of the market. Indeed, Olson (1982) has argued that public sector production may be necessary to compel private sector entrepreneurs to engage in market competition, an argument that is given some support in empirical analyses of the relationship between public sector size and economic growth (Whiteley 1983).

Second, the presumption of government inefficiency has also been attacked, with a number of critics arguing that, at a minimum, the issue of government inefficiency is an open empirical question (Margolis 1981, pp. 181–82). Certainly, the public is uncertain about the efficiency of government. When surveys ask for evaluations of government spending and bureaucratic performance in general, responses tend to be highly critical. But respondents are very supportive of public sector performance when evaluations are sought with reference to specific governmental goods and services (Citrin 1979; Goodsell 1983).

Finally, the value of the efficiency criteria has been questioned as an appropriate standard of evaluation by some commentators. They suggest that it inadequately captures the full dimension of performance characteristics we might desire in social and economic relationships (Margolis 1981, pp. 182–85). Schmid (1978, pp. 241–42), for instance, argues that efficiency is merely a ratio of inputs to outputs and that the real question is one of defining whose inputs and outputs count. The market counts one set of inputs and outputs while the political system may count another. But from Schmid's perspective, both simply represent alternative interpretations of efficiency, rather than one being definitionally efficient, with the other constituting an inefficient outcome.

The supposed freedom advantage of limited government also has attracted critical comment. The most familiar is Galbraith's argument about the real nature of private sector production, as opposed to the idealized image presented by Adam Smith. If the private sector does not operate as a market composed of many small producers, the self-restraining invisible hand vanishes. Private power in the form of monopoly and oligopoly then becomes a serious problem, so serious that any differences between tyrannical private sector power and public sector power may be trivial. This argument is given its most extreme form in neo-Marxist (for example, O'Connor 1973) interpretations that suggest that the public and private sectors are simply alternative vehicles for expressing unrestrained private power.

And similarly to the rejection of efficiency as an unambiguous standard of comparison of the public and private sectors, a number of critics of the conservative critique (Samuels 1976; Samuels and Buchanan 1975; Schmid 1978) have gone so far as to reject the very definition of freedom underlying the libertarian view. The basis of that rejection is the "globalness" of the libertarian definition of freedom as the sum number of opportunities available in a society. As Schmid (1978, pp. 239–40) has stated the question:

> What is meant by the common assertion that the competitive market maximizes freedom? Voluntary trades give the appearance of freedom. If each party did not think he were better off, no trade would take place. Voluntary trade contrasts to government regulation which has the outward appearance of force. But appearances often mask underlying factors of a different sort. . . . The issue is one of whose freedom rather than freedom in the abstract. The great moral choice in any society is whose freedom counts when interests conflict in the face of scarcity.

From this perspective, the real question of freedom is begged by leaving the distribution of income to the market; once shrouded in the sanctity of the status quo, with the necessary assumption that the initial distribution of income was fair to begin with, any current inequality is defined as merely the outcome of individual interactions in the market. With such a set of assumptions, it is easy to foreclose the government from having any role in redistribution.

THE CAUSES OF GOVERNMENT GROWTH

If the conservative critique of big government is derived from the traditional libertarian interpretation of the efficiency and freedom advantages of the market, its assessment of the causes of government growth derive from the newer public choice literature on government and politics. Lacking a positivist view of government, the traditional libertarian perspective could only bemoan the growth of government and encourage limits on that growth; it could not articulate an independent theory of the determinants of public sector size. The positivist view of public choice theory generates a complex theory of the causes of government expansion, a theory usually identified as the *leviathan* or excessive government explanation of government growth (Buchanan 1977; Musgrave 1981; Mueller 1979, pp. 148–70). The explanation is complex; it encompasses a number of different expansion mechanisms under its broad umbrella. These mechanisms include the information monopoly power of bureaucrats (Niskanen 1971), their coercive voting power (Buchanan and Tullock 1977), logrolling behavior between and among elected officials and interest groups (Riker 1980), and fiscal illusions instituted by those officials (Goetz 1977). But at their core, all the mechanisms rest on the notion that government itself is responsible for the growth of government and that changes in the scope of government that occur are unrelated to the objective needs of society. Specifically, pressures for expansion arise from bureaucrats or elected officials who — acting in their own self-interest — call for a larger public sector. Government expansion generated in this manner is a serious threat to the national welfare. "Monopoly rents" collected by bureaucrats or politicians represent resources that could be more efficiently employed in the private sector. Moreover, such expansion of the public sector reduces the scope of the private sector, thereby diminishing economic freedom, and removes the government even further from direct control by the governed by hamstringing any countervailing leverage the market might have on the exercise of public power.

Many other theories purport to account for the expansion of the public sector (for example, see Larkey, Stolp, and Winer 1981; Tarschys 1975), explanations that point to sources outside government in accounting for public sector growth. They have been termed responsive government explanations. These alternative views of the growth process point to such factors as changing public preferences for public and private goods and/or about the distribution of income (Downs 1960, p. 541), the need to meet the capital requirements of industrializing (Wagner 1877) and/or internationally competitive (Cameron 1978) market economies, and other factors. In each case, however, these theories of public sector growth point to objective needs outside government to which government is responding in expanding its activities.

If valid, do these responsive government explanations imply that any particular form of government expansion is absolutely necessary or, alternatively, excessive? Unfortunately the responsive government interpretation is not as conceptually neat as the excessive government model; its answer to this question is necessarily tentative. For unlike the leviathan interpretation, the responsive government answer is not definitionally implicit in the explanations. Instead, whether a particular budgetary item is legitimate or not depends on both the objective need cited for it and the quality of the decision process used to sanction the expenditure. As Musgrave (1983, pp. 57–58) suggests:

> There is no simple way to determine if budgetary activity at any particular time and in any particular place is excessive. The test should be whether or not its prevailing scope is larger than it would be if (1) the democratic process did indeed succeed in expressing the true preferences of the people and (2) this choice were based upon full awareness of all hidden as well as apparent costs and benefits involved.

If the choice processes of government decision making did indeed aggregate informed public preferences about costs (most notably, freedom and efficiency costs) and benefits, then a particular expansion of the scope of government activity is viewed as warranted. Obviously, Musgrave's criteria can only be met in approximation. But his essential point is that each specific increase in the size of government must be evaluated independently of others, an approach that rules out global statements that expansion is inherently too great or harmful.

One important consideration flowing from this responsive government type of evaluation of the government growth process, a consideration that will become increasingly important as we examine the expansion process, is that the specific freedom and efficiency losses associated with each type of expansion need to be carefully specified. The mechanics of government growth posited by the leviathan or excessive government interpretation definitionally involve both freedom and efficiency losses. The same cannot be said for the responsive government explanations. As we will see in more detail as the analysis unfolds, some forms of government expansion envisioned by the responsive government interpretation do not necessarily entail an increase in government activity at the expense of the private sector and, therefore, may not involve the freedom and efficiency losses noted by the conservative critique.

RESTRAINING GOVERNMENT GROWTH

In addition to specifying the causes and consequences of government expansion, the several interpretations of government growth offer implicit advice about both the desirability of restraining the growth of government and the methods such restraint might require. The advice from the excessive government perspective about the appropriateness of limiting government growth is as simple as it is obvious; expansion is, by its nature, excessive and should, therefore, be restricted to preserve the freedom and efficiency advantages of the competitive market.

And if the cause(s) of expansion lie in the government itself, then institutional reforms are needed to constrain the leviathan. These reforms might include the slow starving of the beast through trimming the public sector via conventional budgetary processes (Friedman 1978, pp. 76–81; Boaz 1982; Meltsner 1982; Savas 1982). Such a strategy would involve identifying those activities conducted by government that are more properly conducted in the private sector; the provision and production of public goods and services without demonstrable externality effects would be reduced. And even for those goods where such effects can be demonstrated, public production would not be certain. As Boskin (1982, p. 65) notes, "while private competition may not ensure the most desirable allocation of resources in such circumstances, it is by no means certain that direct government intervention will automatically do better." Government production would be limited to situations where both market failure and relative government success are assured.

But because the institutions of government are in an important sense the cause of the problem in the first place, simple starving of the leviathan through conventional budgetary processes many be inadequate, and more fundamental institutional limitations may be required. Given the conservative critique's diagnosis of the causes of government expansion, it would seem unlikely that public officials would willingly trim the very programs of which they are the primary beneficiaries. As Buchanan (1977, p. 18) notes, "If the bureaucracy is considered to be so firmly entrenched and its institutions so rigid that direct attack would be futile, alternative means may be required." Similarly, Rabushka (1982, p. 340) notes that "growing concern that Congress cannot and will not become a responsible budgetary agency has prompted the current movement to impose a constitutional constraint." Under such conditions, alternative solutions would be required to constrain the growth of government (Aranson and Ordeshook 1981).

Among these alternative solutions are balanced budget proposals (Buchanan and Wagner 1977, 1978; Wagner, et al. 1982), fiscal caps that limit the public sector to some proportion of total economic activity (Wildavsky 1980; Friedman 1978, pp. 14–21), and voter-led referenda on tax limitation (Rabushka and Ryan 1982; Jarvis 1979). Although proponents of the excessive government view continue to debate the relative merits of these proposals, they all address the root causes of government expansion, at least in so far as the leviathan model correctly specified those causes, in a direct and powerful manner, and in a manner that by-passes the institutions that are defined as the source of the problem of excessive government.

As we have seen, the responsive government interpretation offers us much less clear advice on the appropriateness of restraining the expansion of the public sector. Whether such restraint is appropriate depends on a detailed, particularized assessment of the costs and benefits of each case of budgetary expansion, as well as on an evaluation of the decision-making procedures used in sanctioning it. Similarly, the responsive government interpretation has no across-the-board solutions to the problem of government growth. If the causes of expansion lie outside government itself, any solutions will have to be found there. For example, if the cause of expansion lies in the growing investment needs of an industrial society (Wagner 1877), then solutions must be directed to solving that problem.

Although the responsive government interpretation has no across-the-board advice about how best to control government growth, it does suggest that the institutional reforms proposed by the proponents of the conservative critique are strikingly inappropriate. If the responsive government interpretation is correct, the institutional changes would not address the fundamental problems leading to expansion in the first place. The pressures generating government expansion would still be there and would likely be exacerbated if the range and scale of government activities were sharply curtailed. The failure to meet objective social and economic needs would, if they passed the criteria suggested above by Musgrave, entail a loss of efficiency, one of the values presumably being sought by leviathan theorists through institutional limitations on the size of government. Indeed, if government were extremely pressured to respond to unmet social or economic needs, it might be encouraged to circumvent the restrictions imposed upon it (Lowery 1983a, 1983b). And extreme and convoluted circumventions of the limitations could well undermine the openness and legitimacy of our public decision-making institutions (Downs 1980; Olson 1980), a loss that must involve some diminishment of what Friedman means by political freedom, the other value sought by those favoring sharp limits on public sector expansion.

THE ANALYSIS IN OUTLINE

In sum, the conservative critique of big government involves precise views about the consequences and causes of government growth and offers an agenda of solutions to the problem. As we have seen, however, each of these arguments is open to question. How then are we to evaluate the conservative critique as a guide to addressing the problem of government expansion?

Although the critique might be assessed by starting with any one of the three components of its analysis of big government, we believe that a key to assessing its validity lies in evaluating its diagnosis of the causes of government expansion. If the sources of government expansion lie outside government, then the freedom and efficiency costs of government expansion must be evaluated on a program and project basis, rather than be treated as a single, unidimensional phenomenon. Musgrave's criteria, rather than blanket statements couched in the very definition of the problem by the conservative critique of big government, would rule the evaluation of the excessiveness of government growth. Similarly, if support is found for the leviathan interpretation of the causes of government growth, then the institutional reforms that would restrict the fiscal actions of public officials become appropriate solutions to the problem of government expansion. Indeed, they become necessary. But their adoption would be a serious mistake if government grows primarily in response to objective social and economic needs.

The remainder of this book, then, examines the causes of government growth to empirically assess the many different explanations of the expansion process. Through such an examination, we hope to be able not only to evaluate the conservative critique's view of the determinants of public sector size but also to use that evaluation to comment on the contemporary consequences of an expansive public sector and the appropriateness of reforms designed to severely restrict the size of the public sector.

As a first step in our examination, we assess the severity of the problem. How big is the U.S. government and how much has it grown in the postwar era? We address this question in Chapter 2 by examining issues associated with the measurement of government size and growth. Specifically, we contrast the standard indicator of government size used in the empirical literature on government growth — the ratio of total government expenditures to gross domestic product (GDP) measured in current-dollars — with (1) constant-dollar measures that recognize that the cost of providing government goods and services has not grown at the same rate as costs in the private sector and (2) measures that disaggregate total government spending into several component elements.

Chapter 3 then lays the foundation for the examination of the determinants of the size of government by reviewing the many single-factor explanations of the government growth process in the literature and the varied evidence cited in support of each. In Chapter 4, we test a number of these explanations. The explanations are first assessed using the standard measure of government size: government expenditures as a percentage of GDP in current-dollar terms. Although support is found for many of the explanations using this indicator, we argue that substantial measurement error occurs in conventional tests of this type. Then, building on the observations on measurement developed in Chapter 2, we respecify and retest the existing explanations using a more appropriate measure of the dependent variable. Unfortunately, the test using the more valid measure yields very little empirical support for the dominant explanations of government growth.

In Chapter 5, we diagnose the limitations of the existing explanations of public sector expansion; we contend that the failure of these explanations arises from (1) the highly aggregated level at which government expenditures are examined and (2) the excessive reductionism implicit in the various single-factor explanations. We then develop alternatives to these simple explanations based on a disaggregation of the concept of government size. In Chapters 5, 6 and 7, models of public sector size for several components of the size of government are developed and tested. Furthermore, for each component, separate models are built to reflect the excessive government interpretation and the responsive government interpretation. This permits us to assess the relative utility of these two views of public sector expansion.

In the final chapter, in addition to suggesting avenues for further research on government growth, we return to the issues raised here — the conservative critique of big government. That critique's arguments about the causes and consequences of big government — and the solutions for it — are discussed in light of the empirical findings.

2

MEASURING THE SIZE AND GROWTH OF GOVERNMENT

INTRODUCTION

Many claims are made about the excessive size and unnecessary growth of government, especially claims about its dramatic expansion in the post–World War II era. But how do we measure government size and growth? When speaking of the benefits or liabilities of big government, individuals may be referring to many different characteristics of the public sector, including the burden of taxes to support the public sector, the regulatory burden of government, the size of the public budget, the number of public sector employees, and the number of government programs and agencies (Rose 1984; 1983). These many characteristics have all been used, at one time or another, as indicators of the underlying phenomenon of big government and its intrusiveness in our daily lives.

Very likely, however, not one of these indicators fully captures what we mean by big government. Ideally, we would have a summative measure of the concept — intrusiveness of government in private activities — that would capture all of these dimensions of government activity. But constructing such an index would assume that the different dimensions each reflect the same concept — size of government — and this assumption is questionable. For example, many regulations adopted by government that have substantial effects on the economy (for example, civil rights and affirmative action policies) involve only a nominal amount of government expenditure. Moreover, as the existence of deficit financing demonstrates, government taxation does not necessarily match government spending. To a large degree, the spending and revenue choices made by governments are made independently and through different decision-making processes in Congress and state legislatures.

Furthermore, some of these indicators clearly are not tapping into what is typically meant when the issue of big government is raised. That is, some of the indicators suggest that government size has declined or at least remained stable over the last few decades, even as public resentment of big government was building. For instance, the number of laws enacted in the United States has declined over the last five decades (Rose 1984, p. 73). It is, thus, unlikely that this is the specific dimension or aspect of government size that individuals refer to when they speak disparagingly of big government.

How, then, shall we measure government size and growth? Like most previous empirical analyses of the determinants of government size, we employ the ratio of total government expenditures to the size of the economy as a whole — as indicated by gross domestic product (GDP) — as our base measure of the size of the U.S. government. In this chapter, we examine the historical pattern of change in this measure and compare the growth of government in the United States to that of other industrial countries. Additionally, we examine a number of controversies associated with the use of this measure, issues that will become very important in our evaluation of the many explanations of the government growth phenomenon.

THE EXPENDITURE/GDP MEASURE OF GOVERNMENT SIZE

Without question, the ratio of government expenditures to gross domestic product is the most commonly used measure of the size of government. It is certainly the measure that dominates the descriptive literature on government growth (for example, Borcherding 1977b; Nutter 1978; Break 1982; Beck 1981; Ott 1980; Jacobe 1977). And even more important for our purposes, this is the measure most commonly used in empirical tests of the many explanations of the government growth process (for example, Kau and Rubin 1981; Mann 1980; Cameron 1978; Borcherding 1977c), explanations we will review in the next chapter.[1]

That this measure is widely used is not surprising because it has a number of advantages. In addition to being easily quantified, and thus amenable to empirical analysis, the expenditures/GDP ratio facilitates comparisons of the size of government across both time and governments, a considerable advantage when absolute standards for evaluating the appropriate size of government are lacking.

Use of this measure is especially justified, however, given our focus on the conservative critique of big government. Simply put, this measure seems to tap directly what President Reagan and other conservatives mean when they decry the consequences of excessive government; the ratio measure identifies the government's share of the "economic pie," that is, its size relative to the economy as a whole — the focus of the efficiency criteria of the conservative critique of big government.

There is little question using this measure of size that the U.S. government has grown. As seen in Figure 2.1 (constructed from data provided by CITIBASE, a time series data base maintained by Citibank), from 1948 to 1982, total public expenditures — state, local, and federal — as a percentage of GDP has grown from 19.6 percent to 36.1 percent. The rate of growth was most dramatic in the first three decades of this time period, with the government's share of the economic pie growing to 31.8 percent by 1970. During the 1970s, the pace of government growth slowed, leaving the size of government at approximately one-third the size of GDP for the decade. Relative to the size of the economy, then, the government has increased in size by more than 80 percent over the postwar era.

Although this pattern suggests the substantial growth so feared by those who support the conservative critique, the pattern is common to market economies over the postwar period. As seen in Table 2.1, government expenditures as a percentage of GDP have grown in virtually all western European nations — in the case of Sweden and the Netherlands, growing to exceed 50 percent by 1977. In comparison, then, neither the size nor the growth of the government in the United States seems extraordinary. In 1950, the value of the U.S. expenditures/GDP ratio was 93 percent of the average ratio value of 22.9 percent. By 1977, the value of the U.S. ratio was only 82 percent of the average ratio value (40.0). Quite simply, although the U.S. government grew, it grew at a slower rate than the governments of other industrial nations. As seen in the last column of the table, the rate of increase in U.S. government expenditures was only 53 percent from 1950 to 1977. Thus, relative to these other nations, the public sector of the United States was initially small and remains among the smallest even after a period of sustained growth. However, such observations in no way lessen the importance of more systematically examining the determinants of government size. From the perspective of the conservative critique of big government, the dangers of excessive government are still significant to the United States, even if other nations are experiencing even greater difficulties in controlling the growth of their own governments.

MEASUREMENT COMPLICATIONS

While the ratio of government expenditures to Gross Domestic Product serves as our base measure of the size and growth of the public sector, an important caveat to this measurement strategy must be noted. Most analyses of the government growth process employ this simple ratio as a single, summative measure of the size of government in tests of explanations of public sector expansion. This use implies that government growth can be viewed as a unidimensional phenomenon and that all aspects of public sector size can be explained as a single aggregate. This implication is suspect for reasons to be addressed below.

Types of Government Growth

Comparisons of the size of government over extended periods of time (for example, Borcherding 1977a) using the ratio measure has often been criticized. As Margolis (1981, p. 181) has noted, "there remains a need to interpret both parts of the ratio, the data for government as well as gross [domestic] product. The real phenomena underlying these numbers have changed greatly over the same period, casting doubt on a simple and straightforward interpretation of the changing ratios." Specifically, Margolis suggests that changes in the nature of activities that are "marketed" and "unmarketed" significantly undermine simple comparisons of the ratio measure over long periods of time.

More important for our purpose of analyzing the growth of government in the postwar period, such interpretation problems may apply even to relatively short-term assessments. A number of analysts (Beck 1976; 1979; 1981; Ott 1980; Musgrave 1981, pp. 84–87; Break 1982, pp. 40–43) have recently observed that the ratio of government expenditures to GDP may grow for two quite different reasons. First, government may broaden the scale and scope of its activity by increasing the types and amounts of goods and services it provides. Second, the cost of providing a constant level of public sector goods and services relative to the costs of goods and services in the economy as a whole may increase. Growth in the simple ratio of government expenditures to GDP (or growth due to the combined influence of both of these factors) is usually referred to as *current-dollar* (or nominal) growth. Growth purely as a function of increases in the scale and scope of government activity is generally called *real* growth or growth in constant dollars; growth due solely to changing relative costs of public and private sector goods and services is referred to as *cost* growth.

These distinctions have a number of implications for our analysis of the conservative critique of the growth of government. In terms of the hypothesized consequences of big government, the distinction between real- and current-dollar growth suggests the possibility that an increase in the nominal ratio of expenditures to GDP need not lead necessarily to the presumed negative efficiency and freedom consequences of big government. Both of these consequences speak more to relative amounts of resources claimed by the public and private sectors than the costs of these resources. Increasingly expensive public services, however important they are in other respects, do not involve a transfer of activities from the private to the public sector. Therefore, the vitality of the private sector could be unaffected. Indeed, if public sector costs rise more rapidly than those in the private sector, private sector activities would be more attractive relative to competing public sector activities; the private sector option would become increasingly less expensive relative to the public sector option.

Similarly, the distinction between different types of growth has major implications for the analysis of the causes of government growth. That is, most of the extant explanations of government growth speak exclusively to real growth. Some of the explanations attempt to explain cost growth. But none of the dominant explanations of government growth address nominal growth. We will see that this raises a number of specification problems with the existing empirical tests of the many explanations of government growth.

And finally, the distinction has implications for evaluations of the many solutions proposed for the problem of big government. If a major proportion of the expansion of the public sector is a function of changing relative costs of public and private sector activities, then adoption of fiscal limits that severely limit the growth of government expenditures over time would create a situation where the real level of public services would decline over time, even though the nominal level of expenditures remained constant (Baumol 1967). The restrictions imposed by fiscal caps would force government to reduce its activities to finance the growing relative costs of activities it chooses to continue (Lowery 1983a).

Measuring Real Growth

To measure real growth, the numerator and denominator in the ratio of government expenditures to GDP must be adjusted with *implicit price deflators* (IPDs). A price deflator reflects the change over time in the cost of an unchanging market basket of goods and services. When constructing an IPD, one arbitrarily chooses a base year [1972 is used in this study], and, assumes the cost of the market basket in the base year is 100. Then, for each year different from the base year, the IPD is set at the cost of the market basket relative to the base-year cost of 100. To illustrate, if the cost in a given year is 50 percent more than that in the base year, the IPD would take the value 150.

In constructing a deflator for government expenditures, one makes the market basket a representative basket of public sector goods and services; with the GDP deflator, the basket would include both privately and publicly produced output. Although the concept of an IPD is clear, its actual construction for either GDP or government expenditures is complicated by the diverse character of public and private expenditure in the United States (Heller 1981). Thus, to construct the government IPD, for example, public expenditures must be subdivided into components — based upon cost characteristics — deflators must be constructed for each of the components, and then the overall government deflator must be calculated by taking a weighted average of the component IPDs. Break (1982, p. 42) discusses the components typically chosen in his analysis of the need to measure size of government in real terms:

> While many simplistic assumptions are still necessary, different "deflators" are being devised for different types of [government] expenditure. So-called "exhaustive" expenditures (purchases of goods and services) are differentiated from "transfers" (direct payments to individuals in the private sector), and separate adjustment factors are applied to employee compensation and purchases from private firms. The result is a weighted price index that not only makes for a clearer picture of government growth in the United States, but permits comparison with other industrialized countries.

Not surprisingly, the conflicts (for example, Beck 1979; Dubin 1977) that arise over deflation revolve around the simplifying assumptions noted by Break. The most severe of these conflicts arises over the proper deflation of transfer expenditures. But, more recently, the convention of employing the personal (or private) consumption deflator as the appropriate deflator for transfers has become accepted (Heller 1981; Beck 1981). We follow this convention in the analyses that follow.

Do substantive conclusions about the rate of government growth differ when size is measured in real — as opposed to nominal — terms? Figure 2.2 reports annual data for government expenditures as a percentage of GDP where the numerator and denominator are adjusted separately with IPDs (using 1972 as the base year) for the period 1948 to 1982. That is, the CITIBASE data used to construct Figure 2.1 were decomposed into transfers and purchases components, separately deflated with the CITIBASE personal consumption and purchases deflators, and reaggregated to develop a composite measure of real government size. We find a quite different picture from the one drawn by Figure 2.1 once deflated values are employed. Indeed, the growth of government seems to disappear using the real measure in Figure 2.2. During the overall period, the percentage rises slightly from 34.5 percent in 1948 to 36.0 percent in 1982. But for most of the period, the real size of government was decreasing. Although there was a dramatic increase in the percentage to 43.5 percent by 1953, for the remainder of the 1950s and during the 1960s and 1970s, the general trend in the percentage was strongly downward.

And this dramatic difference between real and nominal government growth rates is not one that is confined to the United States. As seen in Table 2.2, the use of deflators to tap the real growth of government significantly reduces the apparent growth of government exhibited by current-dollar measures in all these nations. Whereas the average percentage increase (for the ten nations from 1950 to 1977) in government expenditures as a percentage of GDP is 73 when measured in current-dollar terms, the same average percentage increase in real-dollar terms is only 50.

Disaggregating Government Growth

Even aside from the distinction between real- and current-dollar government growth, clearly not all components of the public sector have expanded at the same rate. Indeed, some components have declined as a percentage of GDP or have remained relatively stable over time. Yet, most specifications of the existing explanations of government growth treat the size of government as an undifferentiated entity, the growth of which can be explained as a single aggregate.

Such an approach is clearly inappropriate. Descriptive analyses of government growth have long noted that different components of public sector activity have had strikingly different growth patterns during the postwar era. For example, consider the distinction between *transfer payments*, in which government provides either cash payments or in-kind benefits directly to individuals, and *purchases* of goods and services, in which government buys resources — both capital and labor — used in producing public services. Several studies note the tremendous growth of the transfer component of government expenditures. In contrast, current-dollar purchases have remained constant or even declined over much of this time period. But even within the purchases component, very different time trends are observed for defense and domestic purchases. Defense purchases have generally declined over the postwar era, especially since the mid-1960s, while domestic purchases have increased, although not at the same rate as transfers (Borcherding 1977a; Tiegen 1980).

These differences in growth rates also appear when one examines government transfers, domestic purchases, and defense purchases as a percentage of GDP. Expenditures in these categories as a percentage of GDP (in current-dollar terms) are presented in Figures 2.3 through 2.5. As shown in Figure 2.3, the transfers share of GDP has had an erratic trend in the postwar era. The transfers share of GDP had a postwar peak in 1949 at 11.8 percent, followed by a sharp dip at the onset of the 1950s. But the transfers share increased throughout the 1950s and during the last part of the 1960s. But it decreased during an intervening period in the early 1960s. The first half of the 1970s saw general stability in the transfers share, followed by a very sharp decrease beginning in 1975.

Figure 2.4 shows that the trend for the domestic purchases share of GDP is similar in some respects to that for transfers. It, too, peaked — at a value of 9.8 percent in 1949 — to be followed by a substantial decrease. But, again, the 1950s and 1960s were generally decades of fairly steady growth in the domestic purchases share. Finally, in sharp contrast to both the transfers and domestic purchases patterns, defense purchases as a percentage of GDP (Figure 2.5) rose in the early part of the period, but has fallen sharply since the early 1950s, only beginning to rise again in the early 1980s.

Like the distinction between the real- and current-dollar size of government, the divergent growth paths of the different components of government expenditures has a number of implications for our analysis of the conservative critique of big government. In terms of the consequences of public sector expansion, growth in transfers (as a share of GDP) has at least two contradictory implications. On the one hand, transfers usually do not involve the public sector performing tasks that could be performed by the private sector. Thus, no direct and specific efficiency loss may arise from production through nonmarket means. On the other hand, however, to the extent that transfers actually redistribute income, they represent redistribution based not on the criteria of the market, but on political criteria. If such redistribution sharply alters the relative ability or willingness of market actors to make certain work or production choices, and if the market's distribution of income is held to be efficient in fully rewarding individual talents and abilities to do what the market values, then the efficiency of the overall economy could be adversely affected.

The conservative critique's evaluation of the causes of government expansion might also be influenced by taking this disaggregated perspective. This is because the many explanations of government growth often allude to processes associated with only one of the components of government expenditures. For instance, Buchanan and Tullock (1977) attribute government expansion to the coercive power of bureaucrats. Certainly, public employees may have an incentive to lobby for increased purchases as such increases could directly benefit them. But it is not at all clear why bureaucrats would want to increase the size of the checks they process for transfer recipients; they would receive no direct benefit from such increases. Thus, although Buchanan and Tullock's hypothesis potentially could explain expansion in purchases, it seems to have little theoretical applicability to transfers.

Disaggregation could also have some implications for the conservative critique's proposed solutions to the problem of government growth. Fiscal caps, balanced budget restrictions, and tax revolts are generally inattentive to the changing relationships between these several categories of expenditure, treating government size as a single, undifferentiated phenomenon. However, if overall government growth largely arises from extraordinary increases in only one of the components of government expenditure, such strategies would represent a blunt and ineffective approach to constraining government growth because they may lead to reductions in many programs for which citizens actually favor increases. Indeed, this very criticism was often heard in evaluations of the Gramm-Rudman-Hollings Act approach to constraining the deficit.

Disaggregating Real Growth

Disaggregation of the components of government growth and the distinction between real- and current-dollar growth interact in an important way. That is, for the same reasons that we calculated the ratio measure of government size in Figure 2.2 using constant dollars, we should also compute the measures of the several disaggregated components of government activity in real terms.

Figure 2.6 presents the time trend of government transfers as a percentage of GDP in real terms. The real transfers share of GDP shows a steadier pattern of increase than the nominal share; the real share continues to increase through the early 1980s in contrast to the nominal share, which turned downward in the mid-1970s. In a similar manner, the pattern of change in the real domestic purchases share of GDP is much steadier than its nominal counterpart. The real domestic purchases share increases gradually from a low in the early 1950s, to reach a peak in 1975. Since 1975, however, the share has been steadily decreasing. In contrast, the shape of the real defense purchases share time trend is quite similar to that of the nominal defense share examined earlier. Both peak in the early 1950s followed by a long period of decline that ends in the late 1970s.

CONCLUSION

In sum, the size of the public sector is not intuitively obvious, nor is its rate of growth over the postwar period; both issues are inextricably intertwined with a series of complex measurement issues reviewed in this chapter. In the next chapter, we begin our examination of the causes of government growth by reviewing the dominant existing explanations of public sector growth. But we address these measurement issues again in Chapter 4 when we test these explanations and, thus, must face squarely the issue of how to measure the dependent variable — size of government.

NOTE

1. Some analysts have used gross national product (GNP) instead of GDP in constructing the measure of government size. GDP is the value of a nation's domestically produced output, while GNP includes, in addition, income from property owned abroad. But the differences in the results of empirical analyses based on these two indicators of the size of the economy would be nominal. We conform to the more common choice in the literature by employing GDP.

Figure 2.1 Total U.S. Government Expenditures as a Percentage of Gross Domestic Product in Current-Dollar Terms, 1948–1982

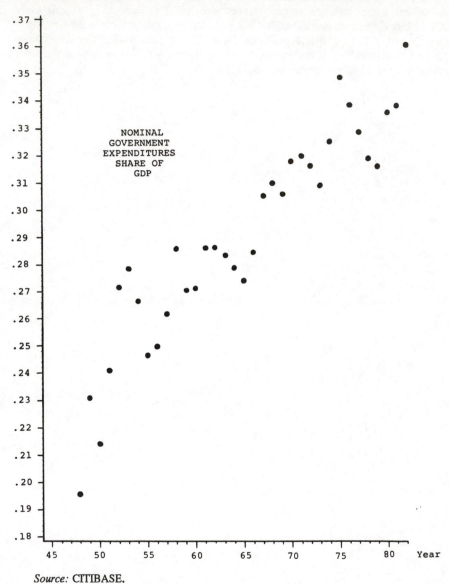

Source: CITIBASE.

TABLE 2.1
Total Government Expenditures as a Percentage of Gross Domestic Product in Current-Dollar Terms for Selected Nations

Country	Year				Absolute Change 1950-1977	Percent Change 1950-1977
	1950	1960	1970	1977		
Austria	21.2	25.6	33.1	39.8	18.6	87.8
Canada	19.0	25.7	32.2	36.9	17.9	94.2
Denmark	18.1	21.7	34.6	n.a.	n.a.	n.a.
France	26.7	30.2	34.7	41.8	15.1	56.6
Germany	28.3	28.2	31.6	41.3	14.6	51.6
Greece	19.6	17.8	22.4	29.0	9.4	48.0
Ireland	23.0	25.0	34.3	n.a.	n.a.	n.a.
Netherlands	23.9	27.8	39.6	52.3	28.4	118.8
Sweden	23.7	26.9	37.1	55.6	31.9	134.6
Switzerland	19.3	17.5	21.3	30.4	11.1	57.5
United Kingdom	30.2	29.0	33.3	40.8	10.6	35.1
United States	21.4	27.1	31.8	32.8	11.4	53.3
Mean	22.9	25.2	32.1	40.0		73.4

n.a.: not available.

Source: CITIBASE for U.S.; Beck (1981) for other nations.

Figure 2.2 Total U.S. Government Expenditures as a Percentage of Gross Domestic Product in Real-Dollar Terms, 1948–1982

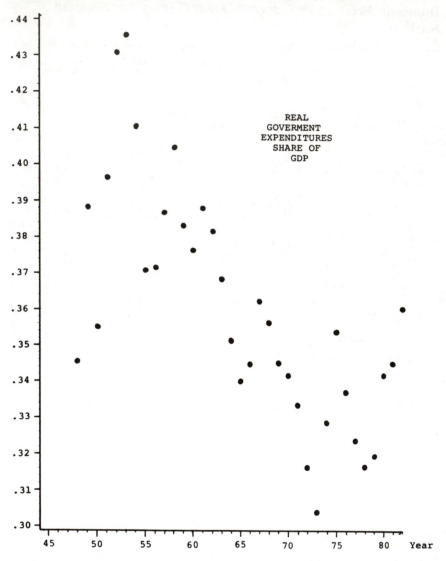

REAL
GOVERMENT
EXPENDITURES
SHARE OF
GDP

Note: Base year for deflators is 1972.

Source: CITIBASE.

28

TABLE 2.2

Total Government Expenditures as a Percentage of Gross Domestic Product in Real-Dollar Terms (1950 Prices) for Selected Nations

Country	Year 1950	Year 1960	Year 1970	Year 1977	Absolute Change 1950-1977	Percent Change 1950-1977
Austria	21.2	23.2	28.7	33.7	12.5	59.0
Canada	19.0	23.8	27.3	32.2	13.2	69.5
Denmark	18.1	20.5	29.2	n.a.	n.a.	n.a.
France	26.7	28.9	32.3	38.5	11.8	44.2
Germany	28.3	27.6	29.6	38.3	10.0	35.3
Greece	19.6	14.2	18.3	24.0	4.4	22.4
Ireland	23.0	25.2	35.2	n.a.	n.a.	n.a.
Netherlands	23.9	26.6	36.4	48.3	24.4	102.0
Sweden	23.7	25.8	32.4	48.1	24.4	103.0
Switzerland	19.3	16.9	21.0	29.4	10.1	52.3
United Kingdom	30.2	27.8	29.8	35.8	5.6	18.6
United States	21.4	22.7	20.6	19.5	-1.9	-8.8
Mean	22.9	23.6	28.4	34.8		49.8

n.a.: not available.

Source: CITIBASE for U.S.; Beck (1981) for other nations.

29

Figure 2.3 Total Transfer Expenditures as a Percentage of Gross Domestic Product in Current-Dollar Terms, 1948–1982

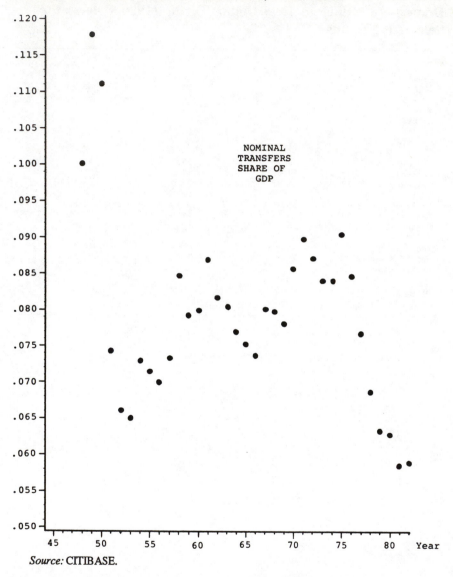

Source: CITIBASE.

Figure 2.4 Total Domestic Purchases as a Percentage of Gross Domestic Product in Current-Dollar Terms, 1948–1982

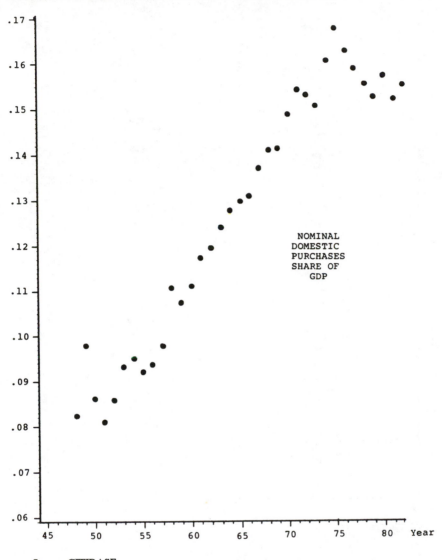

NOMINAL
DOMESTIC
PURCHASES
SHARE OF
GDP

Source: CITIBASE.

Figure 2.5 Total Defense Purchases as a Percentage of Gross Domestic Product in Current-Dollar Terms, 1948–1982

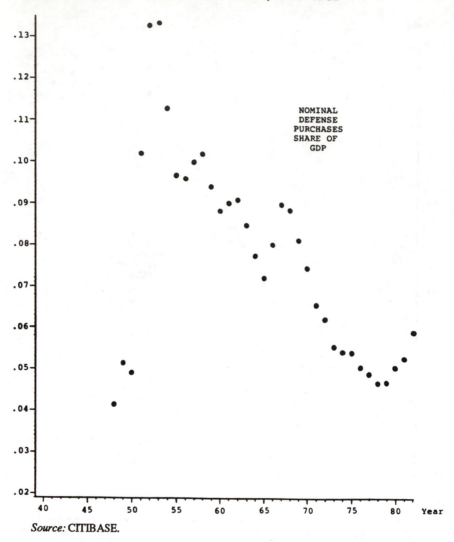

NOMINAL
DEFENSE
PURCHASES
SHARE OF
GDP

Source: CITIBASE.

Figure 2.6 Total Transfer Expenditures as a Percentage of Gross Domestic Product in Real-Dollar Terms, 1948–1982

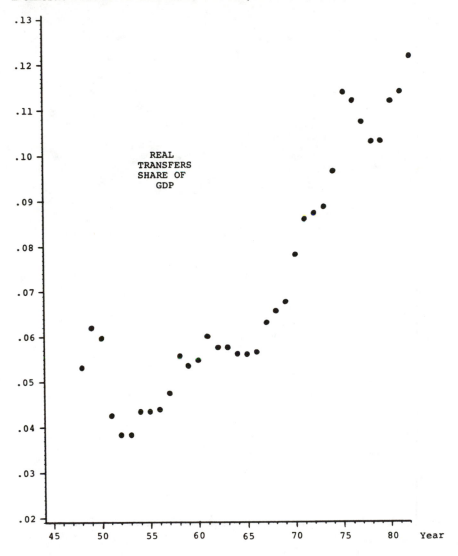

Note: Base year for deflators is 1972.

Source: CITIBASE.

Figure 2.7 Total Domestic Purchases as a Percentage of Gross Domestic Product in Real-Dollar Terms, 1948–1982

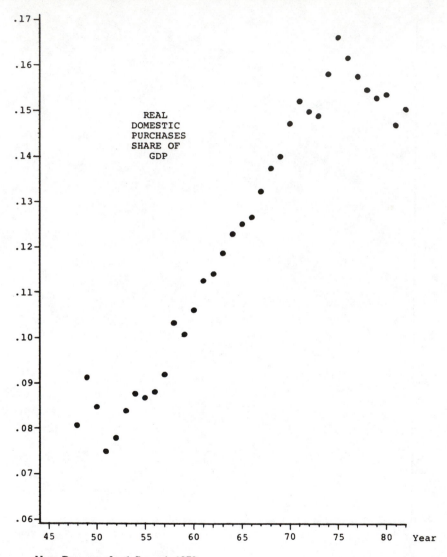

Note: Base year for deflators is 1972.

Source: CITIBASE.

Figure 2.8 Total Defense Purchases as a Percentage of Gross Domestic Product in Real-Dollar Terms, 1948–1982

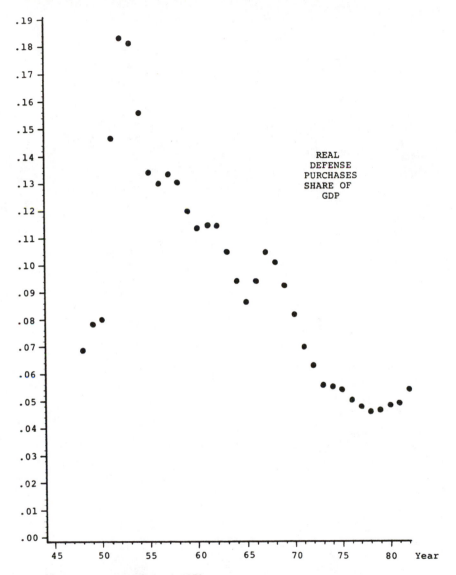

REAL
DEFENSE
PURCHASES
SHARE OF
GDP

Note: Base year for deflators is 1972.

Source: CITIBASE.

II

GOVERNMENT GROWTH: THE LIMITS OF PREVIOUS THEORY AND RESEARCH

3

EXPLANATIONS OF GOVERNMENT GROWTH

THE MANY CAUSES OF PUBLIC SECTOR EXPANSION

Although President Reagan's efforts to constrain the perceived growth of the public sector are only several years old, efforts to understand the process of government growth go back more than a century, to Wagner's Law, first propounded in 1877. Since then, numerous explanations of government growth have been developed (Tarschys 1975; Borcherding 1977b; Larkey, Stolp, and Winer 1981). Some of these explanations are mutually supporting while others are totally inconsistent with one another. Moreover, the empirical evidence marshalled in support of the many explanations ranges from the extremely extensive — as in the case of Wagner's Law — to little or none — as in the case of the "demonstration effect" explanation of government growth. Others are virtually untestable given their formulation. Niskanen's "bureau information monopoly" model, for example, is extremely difficult to test empirically in anything approximating a direct manner (Musgrave 1981, p. 88). Whatever their support, however, these explanations represent the many ways scholars have tried to account for the growth of government. In this chapter, we survey the many explanations and their empirical support.

In developing the survey, we employ an important distinction among the many explanations first suggested by Buchanan (1977), the distinction between responsive government and excessive government explanations of public sector expansion. This distinction is important because the two types of interpretations identify very different sources of

39

government growth, differences that, as we have seen, suggest fundamentally divergent views of the causes and consequences of — and remedies for — government growth. We will return to these differences in the final chapter where the consequences of government growth are discussed in light of our empirical findings.

At their core, the excessive government explanations assume that the choice institutions of government are central to understanding the expansion of the public sector. In some cases, the role of governmental institutions is viewed as mediating the public's demand for governmental services, for example, mediating demand through the competitive party process or through intergovernmental institutions. In such models, as in the responsive government models, the demand for expansion of the public sector is viewed as originating outside the government itself. But importantly, the structure of government has an independent affect on the outcome; government does not simply respond to outside pressures; it mediates them in such a way as to make a given response more or less likely.

In other cases, however, the demand for expansion is viewed as internal to the decision-making institutions of government. In decrying expansion of the public sector, most supporters of the conservative critique of big government point to these versions of the excessive government interpretation. In these models, bureaucrats and politicians are viewed as providing both the demand for as well as the supply of government goods and services. The nature of decision making processes and public institutions becomes central to understanding government growth, then, because the effect of these processes and institutions goes beyond mediating external demands to formulating them.

In contrast, the responsive government explanations view government as a more passive reactor to outside pressures for changes in the scope of government activity. The institutions of government, from this perspective, have little influence on the expansion of government except in so far as they fully and faithfully reflect external pressures calling for government growth. In most of these explanations, some change in technical, social, and/or economic conditions is hypothesized to alter public preferences concerning government production, a change in preferences that is assumed to be reflected automatically in the budget actions of governmental officials. In others, no cause of the public's changing preferences is specified. Instead, some action on the part of the public — such as the election of liberal party candidates — is taken as evidence that preferences have indeed changed. In either case, the unifying factor in all these models is the view of the choice institutions of government as neutral regarding choice outcome.

Following the presentation of the existing explanations of government growth and the evidence cited in support of each, we present a preliminary evaluation of our extant knowledge of government growth. The various theories of the growth process are critically evaluated as a foundation for the empirical tests and theory development to follow.

THE EXCESSIVE GOVERNMENT EXPLANATIONS

In this section, we examine six different explanations, each of which suggests that government has an endogenous role in the determination of public sector size. The first three, the "bureau voting," "fiscal illusion," and "bureau information monopoly" models, represent the most extreme versions of the excessive government interpretations. Each argues that there has been little or no objective reason for public sector expansion, other than the selfish interests of public officials themselves. The last three explanations, the "electoral competition," "interest group," and "institutional centralization" models, view the demands for expansion as coming from outside government but see the structure of political and governmental institutions making it more or less difficult for those demands to be heard and acted upon.

The Bureau Voting Explanation

Like the "interest group" explanation to be presented later, the bureau voting interpretation of the growth of government points to self-interested politics in accounting for the expansion of the public sector. Unlike that model, however, this explanation finds bureaucrats rather than their clients (in concert with bureaucrats) the culprits. The key to this explanation is the coercive voting power of public employees; "as government employees become a larger share of the work force, they have more and more to say about who wins elections and they are able to forge explicit and implicit contracts about their own wages" (Courant, Gramlich, and Rubinfeld 1979; see also Buchanan and Tullock 1977; Buchanan 1977). Bureaucrats, interested in their own wages and the perks and promotion advantages of a growing bureaucracy, are hypothesized to vote in a single block for political candidates willing to promise support for public employees.

Although the self-interest base of this explanation is plausible, most of the empirical support for this explanation remains indirect, including observations of dynamic collinearity between levels of public spending in the United States and levels of public employment. Still, we have long known that public employees are somewhat more liberal than the population as a whole, if not greatly so (Meier 1975; Aberbach and Rockman 1976). And public employees do turn out to vote at higher rates than other segments of the population (Bush and Denzau 1977). But more direct examinations of bureaucratic voting behavior on issues that would be expected to be very close to bureaucratic interests, including tax revolt referenda issues, have failed to uncover the clear patterns of self-interest voting that this explanation leads us to expect. Moreover, a direct bureau self-interest in growth in all components of government expenditures is not evident. Bureaucrats would seem to have a direct interest in expanding government purchases because this category of expenditure includes their wages, but there is no apparent direct tie between bureaucratic self-interest and the size of the transfer checks they issue. And, as is clear from Figures 2.6, 2.7, and 2.8, growth in the transfers component of government expenditures accounts for a substantial portion of public sector expansion in the postwar period.

In formalizing this explanation of the growth of government, Courant, Gramlich, and Rubinfeld (1979) draw our attention directly to the size of the public employee population relative to the voting age population (also see Buchanan and Tullock 1977, p. 148). Therefore, we can specify this interpretation of the growth of government with the equation

$$SIZE_t = A + B_1 \, GOVEM_{t-1} \qquad\qquad (3.1)$$

where **SIZE** is the size of the public sector in year t, **GOVEM** is the size of the public employee voting block — the number of government employees as a percentage of the voting age population — in the previous year, and A is the intercept.[1] Coefficient B_1 should be greater than zero, indicating that the size of the bureau voting block is positively related to the size of the public sector.

The Fiscal Illusion Explanation

The explanation of government growth rests on a complex causal chain, one suggesting that political elites systematically manipulate public preferences for government expenditures. They do so by adopting revenue collection mechanisms that lead voters to systematically underestimate the costs of public sector goods and services and, therefore, demand more than an optimal level. At its core, the explanation rests on the twin notions of "rational ignorance" on the part of voters and "electoral maximization" on the part of officials, theoretical premises that are commonly used in public choice analyses of governmental institutions (Downs 1957; Goetz 1977; Pommerehne and Schneider 1978; Bartlett 1973). Politicians play on the rational ignorance of voters by adopting revenue mechanisms that enable them to escape the dilemma inherent in "the tenuous relationship between what citizens want and what they pay" (Meltsner 1971).

Although plausible, each step of the causal chain underlying the fiscal illusion explanation can be and has been challenged. The first proposition of the argument is that politicians actually manipulate fiscal instruments in the pursuit of electoral advantage, a proposition that immediately confronts the social and economic constraints that govern tax policy (Bingham, Hawkins, and Herbert 1978) as well as the institutional forces of incrementalism (Witte 1982). Second, the model implies that voters respond to this manipulation by underestimating tax burdens. But given the high absolute degree of tax ignorance on the part of the public (Hansen 1983), it might well be argued that specific tax structures have little additional impact on miscalculations of tax burdens. And third, the explanation implies that voters then demand greater expenditures, a proposition that relies on the dubious assumptions that voters accurately estimate the benefits of public spending (Downs 1960) and weigh taxes against expenditures in cost-benefit calculations (Hansen 1983, p. 195). If any of these steps in the chain collapses, the whole illusion argument falls.

But beyond the need to satisfy a complex causal chain, the illusion explanation is difficult to evaluate given the lack of any agreement on precisely what revenue collection mechanisms are illusionary. Virtually every type of revenue mechanism has been identified as illusionary in some way (Lowery 1985; Goetz 1977). This multiplicity undermines the illusion explanation because, if all or nearly all revenue mechanisms are illusionary, it is difficult to see how politicians could render the system more illusionary by moving from one tax mechanism to another; fiscal illusion would be a constant. As such, the illusion construct might still be operative, but it could not account for changes in the size of the public sector.

Still, the illusion explanation is frequently employed to explain the growth of government (Goetz 1977; Pommerehne and Schneider 1978; Hansen 1977), with tax withholding (Enrick 1963; Wagstaff 1965), deficit financing (Buchanan and Wagner 1977; Vickrey 1961), high revenue elasticity (Hansen and Cooper 1980; Formouzis and Puri 1980; Craig and Heins 1980), a complex tax system (Wagner 1975; Bartlett 1973), and indirect taxation (Wildavsky 1975; Cameron 1978) often identified as illusion inducing mechanisms.

Although the problem of specifying precisely which fiscal mechanisms are illusionary will be addressed more thoroughly when we test the illusion explanation in Chapter 4, for now we can formalize the explanation in the following manner:

$$SIZE_t = A + B_1 \, ILLUSION_{t-1} \tag{3.2}$$

where **ILLUSION** is the degree of illusion evidenced in revenue collection mechanisms. The coefficient B_1 would be expected to be positive, indicating that highly illusionary fiscal structures are associated with a larger public sector.

The Bureau Information Monopoly Model

Next to Wagner's Law, the bureau information monopoly model has been studied more than any other explanation of the growth of government. And the attention given it rivals that directed to Wagner's Law despite its being only slightly more than a decade old whereas Wagner's Law has been the subject of scholarly scrutiny for over a century. As developed by William Niskanen (1971) in *Bureaucracy and Representative Government*, this explanation rests on the twin assumptions that bureaucrats are budget maximizers and that in their relationships to legislatures, they can be viewed as perfectly discriminating monopolists. Budget maximizing incentives and perfect control of information, it is then demonstrated, lead to collection of monopoly rents on the part of bureaucrats, rents that result in excessive government budgets. Although Niskanen's model has been reformulated in numerous ways (see Orzechowski 1977; Mueller 1979), his core assumptions of information monopoly and budget maximization remain at the heart of most economic models of bureaucracy. While much indirect evidence is cited in support of this model (see Borcherding 1977b), most of its support arises from sophisticated analytic demonstrations devoid of empirical content.

And despite the attention given this model, it remains theoretically suspect for a number of reasons. First, although it is difficult to argue that budget maximizing behavior is not a part of the content of bureau self-interest, that content is surely broader than budget maximization alone. Downs (1966), for instance, identifies a broad array of bureaucratic goals, some of which conflict strongly with maximizing budgets with naked abandon. Moreover, a recent empirical assessment finds little support for the notion that bureaucrats uniformly pursue budget maximization (Sigelman 1986). Similarly, the model implies that legislators are, to use Musgrave's (1981, p. 94) characterization, "imbeciles," willingly agreeing with the bureaucrats, a characterization that is inconsistent with what we know about appropriation committee norms and specialization (Fenno 1966).

More important, the institutional context implicit in Niskanen's model is so weak as to raise serious questions of external validity. For instance, the role of the executive is totally ignored in the Niskanen model, a source of serious misspecification given the budget-cutting fervor of the Nixon Office of Management and Budget (OMB) (Berman 1979), not to mention that of OMB under David Stockman (Nathan 1983). Indeed, administrative reforms over the past two decades have given the president even more influence in the budgetary process; the "bubble-up" process of budget construction that allowed full play of budgetary acquisitiveness has been replaced with a "top-down" process that emphasizes executive control (Kamlet and Mowery 1980).

Similarly, the model assumes that the bureaucracy is a monolith with little or no competition, a result that is inconsistent with many interpretations of intragovernmental politics (Brenton and Wintrobe 1982; Huntington 1961). Indeed, at least some analyses of bureaucratic control emphasize the problem of excessive competition rather than the problem of monolithic bureaucratic control (Yates 1982).

Perhaps even more devastatingly, Miller and Moe (1983) have turned Niskanen's analysis on its head by pointing out that if the bureaucracy is a monopolist, then Congress is certainly a monopsonist. Under such conditions, the bargaining positions of Congress and the bureaucracy would be quite different from that suggested by Niskanen, with the advantage flowing to the Congress. In sum, while this model is one of the most discussed models of government growth, it has the weakest theoretical and empirical foundation of any of them.

The lack of empirical foundation is not surprising given the analytical foundations of the model. It is very difficult, if not impossible, to measure the extent to which government bureaus control information at a given time. Accordingly, we will not be able to test this model when we turn to empirical analysis in Chapter 4. Still, for comparison purposes, we can formalize this model in the following manner:

$$SIZE_t = A + B_1 \, MONOP_{t-1} \qquad\qquad (3.3)$$

where **MONOP** is the degree to which information is controlled by government bureaus. The coefficient B_1 would be expected to be positive indicating that greater bureau monopoly of information is associated with a larger public sector.

The Electoral Competition Explanation

Dating to V. O. Key (1949), the electoral competition explanation of the expansion of public expenditures is one of the oldest and most studied in political science. As Key argued, under conditions of strong party competition, the political "outs" will have an incentive to offer government benefits to the "have-nots" of society in order to build a majority electoral base. This is because the poor constitute the largest pool of potential — but as yet unmobilized — voters. We should find, then, that government programs for the poor expand — and, thus, government grows — under more competitive electoral conditions (Gray 1976, p. 239). Despite its pedigree, however, the competition interpretation has not garnered wide support. Although it has been challenged theoretically (Jennings 1979), the most significant shortcoming of the explanation is the poor empirical support for it in the literature (for example, Dawson and Robinson 1963; Dye 1966; Sharkansky 1967; for more supportive evidence, if under restrictive conditions, see Fry and Winters 1970).

More recently, however, a number of analysts have emphasized the interactive role of interparty competition and the frequency of elections in influencing government spending. Specifically, if the competition hypothesis holds, that it is based on electoral incentives should lead us to expect that it would be more relevant at times immediately before an election than at times when an election is a long time away. Only in periods before elections would politicians have an incentive to choose or promise policies designed to broaden an electoral base. Support for this reinterpretation of the competition hypothesis can be found in the "political business cycle" (Tufte 1978; Keech 1980; Kiewiet and McCubbins 1985) and state tax adoption (Mikesell 1978) literatures that find substantial "timing of election" effects on macroeconomic policies and patterns of tax adoption respectively. To date, the effect of the frequency of elections on government growth has been tested only on a cross-national basis, and only with modest results (Cameron 1978).

In any event, a formal specification of this explanation must assume not only that a high level of interparty competition and the presence of an election should encourage a larger public sector, but also that the level of interparty competition and the presence of an election should interact in influencing the amount of change in the size of government. In particular, interparty competition should have a stronger effect on government activity during an election year than in a nonelection year. Accordingly, we develop the following formalization of the electoral competition explanation:

$$SIZE_t = A + B_1 \, SIZE_{t-1} + B_2 \, ELECT_t + B_3 \, COMP_{t-1}$$
$$+ B_4 \, [(ELECT_t)(COMP_{t-1})] \tag{3.4}$$

where $ELECT_t$ is a dichotomous variable that equals 1 if an election is held in year t and 0 otherwise and $COMP$ indicates the level of interparty competition. All slope coefficients are expected to be positive with B_1 equal to 1.[2]

The Interest Group Explanation

The role of interest groups in encouraging government expansion has received increased attention in recent years (Peltzman 1980; Wildavsky 1979). Often based on a public choice (Downs 1957; Tullock 1977) model of the political process, the interest group explanation suggests that elected officials have electoral incentives that lead them to serve particularized groups, while the various interests themselves have incentives to court a tragedy of the commons outcome via logrolling.

According to Riker (1980, p. 89), one outcome of uncontrolled interest group influence "is a result we see in nearly every country, a huge long-term growth in the public sector." Wildavsky (1980, p. 42) has identified this as the "Pogo Principle" of public expenditure growth: "we have met the enemy and he is us."[3] Strong, if indirect, evidence for this interpretation is found in the dramatic growth of transfers — especially to senior citizens, farmers, veterans, and welfare recipients — that have outpaced growth in the other components of government expenditure for much of the postwar period (Borcherding 1977b; Tiegen 1980; Muller 1984).

However, the evidence for the Pogo Principle is far from complete. Research on the budgetary process still emphasizes the "guardian of the public purse" interpretation of congressional decision making on expenditures, an interpretation given an executive focus in the budget-cutting efforts of President Reagan as his second term began (Fenno 1966). Moreover, Downs (1960) has argued that the growth of particularized government benefits is more than offset by underproduction of genuine collective consumption goods, goods for which groups interested in particularized benefits would have little concern. And several studies have failed to uncover any pattern of self-interest based voting in elections where it should be most obvious if this explanation of the growth of government were accurate (Mariotti 1978; Citrin 1979; Kau and Rubin 1979).

The key to formalizing this explanation is identifying the sizes of the groups benefiting — or more accurately, potentially benefiting — from particularized public sector spending. We will discuss the difficulties involved in measuring this in the next chapter. For now, though, we formalize this explanation with the following model:

$$\text{SIZE}_t = A + B_1 \text{ INTEREST}_{t-1} \tag{3.5}$$

where **INTEREST** represents the strength of interest groups desiring particularized public spending. Coefficient B_1 should be positive.

The Institutional Centralization Explanation

Another explanation of government expansion points to the level of institutional centralization of political decision making to account for the expansion of government. Cameron (1978) presents the typical form of this interpretation, arguing that highly centralized governments are better able to constrain the growth of government than are decentralized governments. Simply put, more highly centralized governments are more likely to directly balance the spending and taxing functions of government. When there are numerous governmental levels, such fiscal mechanisms as revenue sharing and intergovernmental aid lead to situations with the government responsible for spending public funds different from that responsible for raising the funds in the first place. Under such conditions, the inherent exchange relationship between taxing and spending disappears, with the recipient level of government more likely to spend than it would be if it had raised the funds itself (Heidenheimer 1975, p. 28; Goetz 1977; for a constrasting view, see McKenzie and Staff 1978).

Additionally, others have argued that decentralized governments are more likely to respond positively to demands for government growth because such decentralization provides more access points for those favoring expansion (Grodzins 1960). For instance, proponents who have failed to persuade the national government to adopt their program could pursue adoption at the state and local levels.

Finally, decentralized governments not only might be more open to those favoring increased public expenditures; decentralization also creates a new set of claiments on the national government — the lower-level governments. State and local governments may respond to spending demands by providing funding themselves or by lobbying the central government for increased aid (Haider 1974; Aranson and Ordeshook 1981, p. 171).

While this explanation has wide currency, it is also subject to both empirical and theoretical challenges. Empirically, Cameron's (1978) cross-national test of this model finds that degree of government decentralization is negatively associated with government expansion, the opposite that would be expected according to this explanation. And on the theoretical front, it would seem reasonable to expect that if the spending level of government's incentives to spend are greater under decentralized arrangements, the taxing level of government's incentive to tax would also be reduced; in such a situation, that level of government would receive all the political blame for higher taxes but none of the political credit for higher spending. Moreover, if a decentralized government has more access points for those favoring expansion of government, it also must have more veto points useful to those favoring limiting the size of government.

This explanation is difficult to formalize in the U.S. setting because the level of centralization, at least in so far as formal institutional arrangements are concerned, is a constant. Still, the United States has evolved a number of new institutional arrangements over the postwar period — including revenue sharing and other forms of intergovernmental aid — that have created new opportunities for separating the taxing and spending functions (Reagan and Sanzone 1981; Sundquist 1969). Therefore, we formalize this explanation in the following manner:

$$SIZE_t = A + B_1 \, DECENT_{t-1} \qquad\qquad (3.6)$$

where **DECENT** is the level of fiscal decentralization of the governmental system. According to the hypothesis, we should find that the level of decentralization is positively related to the size of the public sector (that is, $B_1 > 0$).

THE RESPONSIVE GOVERNMENT EXPLANATIONS

The seven responsive government explanations all point to conditions, external to government, that in some way necessitate government expansion. The first and most general is Wagner's Law that points to a number of aspects of industrialization in accounting for government expansion. Although less general, the next two explanations, the "international" and "supply-side" explanations, also focus on the impact of changing economic conditions. In contrast, the "party control," and "demonstration effect" explanations suggest that the changing preferences of the public can account for government expansion. Finally, the "concentration-displacement" model points to the interaction of public preferences and incrementalism in explaining public sector growth.

Wagner's Law

The oldest and most cited explanation of the growth of government points to the forces inherent in industrialization in explaining the expansion of the public fisc: Wagner's Law of Rising Public Expenditures. Suggested by German economist Adolph Wagner (1877) more than a century ago, Wagner's law has been the subject of numerous theoretical interpretations, reinterpretations, and empirical tests. The law points to three aspects of the process of industrialization, each of which is hypothesized to lead to government growth (Mann 1980, p. 189).

The first of these concerns the income elasticity of public expenditures. Simply put, Wagner's Law posits an income elasticity greater than one. That is, many public goods and services are viewed as luxury goods, goods that are demanded only after an individual's private needs are met. Examples of such luxury public goods might include public parks or, to use a more recent application of Wagner's Law, clean air (Thurow 1980, 103–12). As incomes grow as a function of expanding industrialization, Wagner would suggest that citizens demand more of these public goods, demands that lead to an expansion of the public sector.

This aspect of the law has been extensively tested in efforts to determine the elasticity of public spending (Mann 1980; Borcherding 1977c) and the generalizability of the law across varying levels of industrialization (Bird 1971, p. 19; Mann 1980; Musgrave 1969, pp. 112–13; Gupta 1968; Wildavsky 1975, pp. 234–35). At the same time, however, a number of analysts, most notably Downs (1960) and Galbraith (1958), have raised serious questions about the operation of the law in advanced industrial nations where, it is argued, advertising for private goods and the multiplicity of public goods undermine the simple relation between income and the demand for public goods and services posited by Wagner.

Beyond the income elasticity of public expenditures, industrialization is assumed to influence government growth through the inherent expansion of societal interdependencies in industrial societies. Borcherding (1977b, p. 52) summarizes this component of Wagner's Law when he notes that, "As the economy develops and its population becomes larger, more densely settled, and more urbanized, types of interdependencies develop that are not well handled by private markets. Under these conditions, governmental solutions may become appealing." To use a simple example, as industrialization leads to urbanization, the interdependency problem of traffic jams develops and leads to the governmental solution of traffic lights. Although the precise specification of this effect is subject to varying interpretations, this aspect of Wagner's Law has been used frequently in conventional economic (Fabricant 1952; Musgrave and Culberton 1953), political science (Sharkansky 1967; Dye 1966), and neo-Marxist analyses (O'Connor 1973, pp. 150–78) of public sector growth.

The final element of Wagner's Law points even more directly to the process of industrialization in explaining the growth of government. As Mann (1980, p. 189) has stated it, "the technological needs of an industrial economy require larger amounts of capital than are forthcoming from the private sector. Therefore, the state has to provide the necessary capital funds to finance large-scale capital expenditures." That is, the state becomes a partner in financing the growth of industrialization, a partnership that necessitates government growth. In part, this partnership is reflected in public expenditures for the infrastructure needed for industrial development, including the complex technologies associated with communications and transportation. But it includes more direct contributions as well, contributions fully reflected in the recent diversification of state government tax policies under competition for business expansion and location (Harrison and Kanter 1980). Although most governments have grown as a result of this partnership as Wagner's Law would lead us to expect, the Wagner's Law interpretation of this phenomenon has been challenged. Specifically, neo-Marxists have argued that these partnership activities represent less a response to objective needs than to "monopoly capital's desire" to externalize production costs (O'Connor 1973, pp. 97–123).

In any event, we can formalize this explanation of the government growth process in the following manner:

$$SIZE_t = A + B_1 \, INCOME_{t-1} + B_2 \, INTERDEP_{t-1} + B_3 \, INDUS_{t-1} \qquad (3.7)$$

where **INCOME** is the total level of personal income, **INTERDEP** is the level of societal interdependencies, and **INDUS** is the level of industrialization. All three slope coefficients are hypothesized to be positive, indicating that higher values of each are associated with a larger public sector.

The International Explanation

One of the major economic changes of the postwar era must certainly be the growing internationalization of market economies. And while this internationalization has generated new sources of competition that should lead to greater economic efficiencies, it has also exposed the domestic economies of the advanced industrial countries to new sources of instability. David Cameron (1978) has built on the work of a number of other analysts (for example, Lembruch 1977; Lindbeck 1976; Krasner 1976) to suggest that this exposure, and the problems thereby generated, are major sources of government growth.

From the perspective of this model, the role of dependence on international trade becomes critical to the extent that it weakens domestic control of the macroeconomy. Domestic monetary and fiscal controls, which primarily influence domestic sources of instability, would be less effective in controlling macroeconomic instability. As dependence on international trade increases, then, the economy could become increasingly vulnerable to imported inflation, unemployment, and the other ills of advanced market systems. This, in turn, is hypothesized to lead to greater demands for an expansion of government activity in the form of a "new state mercantilism" designed to "dampen the effects of the open economy on production, employment, and consumption" (Cameron 1978). Government is asked to control the economy in new ways, including ways that necessitate an expansion of governmental activity, to control economic instability arising from dependence on international trade.

While Cameron (1978) has found some support for this model in cross-national analyses of government growth, this model, like the others, is obviously incomplete. Aside from the inadequacy of cross-sectional testing of dynamic hypotheses, this explanation seems inconsistent with recent U.S. experience. For instance, U.S. economic dependence on foreign trade increased markedly in the 1970s, just as government growth was leveling off (Ott 1980; Shannon 1981). Even more paradoxically, the massive increase in U.S. trade dependence under the Reagan administration accompanied the most determined efforts to cut the growth of government in the postwar era. Nevertheless, the formal specification of this model is very direct:

$$SIZE_t = A + B_1 \, TRADE_{t-1} \qquad\qquad (3.8)$$

where **TRADE** is the level of dependence on international trade, and B_1 is expected to be positive.

The Supply-Side Explanation

Unlike the previous explanations that focus on forces leading to greater demand for public expenditures, the supply-side explanation assumes that the level of demand is constant. What changes to accommodate government growth is, instead, the supply of revenue available to meet that demand. As Kau and Rubin (1981, p. 261) noted, "if the demand for government spending has not changed, [an] increase in supply [of revenue] would lead to a larger public sector." Such changes in supply, they suggest, result from economic changes that make more personal income subject to taxation.

And, according to Kau and Rubin, a number of changes have taken place in the U.S. economy in the postwar period that should have led to an increase in revenue, most of which involve the integration of workers formerly employed outside the taxable-wage system of employment into that system. Specifically, they suggest that greater female labor force participation has increased revenue supply as more women earn income that is more easily subject to taxation. Similarly, the decline in farm employment and self-employment — occupations where hidden income and bartering make direct taxation difficult — should have raised the supply of revenue. But beyond tapping into labor activity that was formerly beyond the reach of the "tax man," they suggest that the shift from noncorporate to corporate firm arrangements should have generated revenue increases because of the greater stringency of corporate income reporting requirements. As Kau and Rubin note, "there is a higher effective rate of taxation on corporate income." With changing labor and business markets, then, the government supposedly reaped a windfall of new revenue that enabled it to grow in response to omnipresent demands for public spending.

Although Kau and Rubin find some empirical support for this model for the United States in the postwar period, the model hardly tells a complete story of public sector growth in the United States. For instance, despite the presumed government interest in growing revenue and the windfall it was presumed to garner from the expansion of corporate firm arrangements, corporate tax rates were steadily cut throughout the postwar era (McIntyre and Tipps 1983). Similarly, personal income tax rates were regularly cut on a near biannual (to coincide with congressional elections, of course) basis from 1964 through 1976, an action that is difficult to understand if government officials were interested in using any revenue windfalls to meet the constant demands for more spending. In short, many other tax-policy actions taken during this time period seem totally inconsistent with the underlying logic of this explanation.

Still, we can formalize this explanation of public sector expansion with the following model:

$$SIZE_t = A + B_1 \, TAXABLE_{t-1} \tag{3.9}$$

where **TAXABLE** indicates the extent to which the organization of economic activity renders income easily taxable. The coefficient B_1 is expected to be positive.

The Party Control Explanation

The party control explanation of the growth of government, among all those considered here, is probably the one most consistent with "textbook" interpretations of representative government. At its core, this explanation assumes that citizen-voters' preferences for government goods and services change over time and that their preferences are fully reflected in and represented by their electoral choices. As Anthony Downs (1960, p. 541) states, "the division of resources between the public and private sectors is roughly determined by the electorate." When the public prefers more public goods and services, this preference would lead to greater support for liberal political parties and candidates, and when they prefer less government, that preference should be reflected in support for conservative parties (Schumpeter 1950). Party control would represent a mandate to either expand or contract the size of government.

Of course, this explanation makes some rather tenuous assumptions about voters, political parties, and the decision-making institutions of government. Voters are assumed to view politics in much the same way that rational consumers are assumed to approach market transactions. They are assumed to have firm preferences and to rationally chose among the packages of goods and services offered by political parties. But, the public's preferences for public goods and services have remained fairly constant throughout the postwar period, and seem to be unrelated to political party affiliation or ideological identification (Lowery and Sigelman 1982). Moreover, the political ballot is a remarkably poor instrument of expressing such preferences, especially in comparison to the "dollar ballots" of the market (Buchanan 1954). Just as paradoxically, the frequent similarity of political party platforms designed to meet the preferences of the median voter (Downs 1957, p. 117) and the increasingly weak linkage between partisanship and congressional voting

(Niemi and Weisberg 1976, p. 239) suggest that parties are less than ideal vehicles to represent citizen preferences, even assuming that those preferences are very sharp and organized along partisan lines. And the institutions of budget decision making through which citizen preferences are presumed to be represented by elected officials have long been described as being dominated by a form of "institutional" rather than "partisan" politics (Davis, Dempster, and Wildavsky 1966; Wildavsky 1964; Fenno 1966). In sum, the foundations of this textbook interpretation are tenuous at best.

It should not be surprising, then, that the party control explanation has received only modest support in studies of state government spending (for example, Dye 1966; Fry and Winters 1970; Winters 1976; Jones 1974; Marquette and Hinkley 1981). Indeed, Wanat (1978, p. 114) has argued that, "unlike much government activity, party is not central to understanding budgeting."

Still, political scientists have not accepted this conclusion and continue to insist that party control should matter. And numerous case studies (for example, Fisher 1975; Ippolito 1981, pp. 174–75) continue to find some evidence of partisan effects. Moreover, more recent empirical tests have found party control to matter in ways more subtle than those investigated in the empirical analyses cited above. Liberal party control does matter, if at the margin (Pjerrou-Desrouches 1981). More important for our purposes, party control has been found to influence government spending in cross-national tests (Cameron 1975) and during periods of transition of party control of government in the United States (Davis, Dempster, and Wildavsky 1974).

We formalize the party control explanation in the following manner:

$$SIZE_t = A + B_1 \, PARTY_{t-1} \qquad\qquad (3.10)$$

where **PARTY** indicates the degree of liberal party control of government, and B_1 is hypothesized to be positive.

The Concentration-Displacement Explanation

As developed by Peacock and Wiseman (1961), the concentration-displacement explanation of the growth of government points to the influence of crises on citizens' expectations about the appropriate size of government. At any given time, it is argued, citizens will have a set of expectations that define the share of economic activity that is appropriate for government: a government spending X percent of GDP is tolerable, whereas X+1 percent would be intolerable. In the face of crises, however, they modify their expectations. In the case of war or serious depression, government growth is acceptable to face the temporary threat to the nation. But having then experienced government activity beyond their previous threshold level of tolerability and having experienced no untoward consequences, citizens are then hypothesized to adjust the threshold of tolerability upward. Government's share of the economic pie may decline after the threat but not to its precrisis level. This new level then defines the acceptable limit of government activity until the next crisis occurs.

This explanation of public sector expansion seems to account for U.S. government growth for most of this century as sharp increases in public sector size accompanied both world wars, the depression, and the Korean conflict (for an alternative interpretation, see Borcherding 1977a). The explanation breaks down for most of the postwar period, however, as the domestic budget growth associated with the Johnson Great Society programs was associated not with a domestic economic crisis, but with the longest period of sustained economic growth over the whole period. Also contrary to expectations, defense expenditures declined during most of the Vietnam War period.

A modified form of the concentration-displacement explanation is consistent with the incremental model of budgeting (Wildavsky 1964; Davis, Dempster, and Wildavsky 1966). Importantly, however, this modified interpretation points to the operation of the choice institutions of government, rather than to citizen preferences about public spending, in explaining the growth of government. As such, it has characteristics of both the responsive government and excessive government interpretations.

Specifically, the incremental budgeting model suggests that the complexity of budget calculations leads to a rational strategy of ignor-ing the base in budget decisions and thus avoids reconsidering programs included in previous budgets. If these programs were adopted in the face of specific crises, they would then persist in the budget long after the crisis disappeared. This type of argument has been used to explain the growth of bureaucracies and their survival long after the crisis that led to their birth disappeared (Kaufman 1976). And Beck (1981) has argued that transfer payments grow in response to business cycle fluctuations — a form of economic crisis when the cycle carries the economy into a recession — in the ratchetlike manner suggested by this interpretation.

Given the combined incremental/crisis interpretation of this model, we offer the following formalization:

$$SIZE_t = A + B_1 \, SIZE_{t-1} + B_2 \, CRISIS_t \tag{3.11}$$

where **CRISIS** is a measure of the presence (and the severity) of crisis conditions — equaling zero in the absence of crisis and a number greater than zero when a crisis exists. The prediction is that B_1 equals one and B_2 is positive. Unlike the independent variables in most previous explanations, **CRISIS** is not lagged behind the dependent variable because crises, such as war, are likely to prompt immediate increases in government spending.

The Demonstration Effect Explanation

Like the concentration-displacement explanation, the demonstration effect explanation rests on notions of citizen beliefs about the tolerable limits of some aspect of government or society. But in this case, the focus of the citizen's concern is not the size of government per se, but the level of inequality in the society. As Tarschys (1975) has presented this interpretation of government growth, any society is assumed to tolerate a given level of income or regional inequality. The actual level of inequality may differ sharply from that level, but if information about the gap between the actual and tolerable levels is absent, little redistribution will be undertaken. The key, then, is the level of information about that gap. If it increases, redistributive efforts, and hence an expansion of government activities, would be expected. Such information would presumably increase both the demand for redistribution (Jennings 1980) on the part of the poorer class and the willingness of the wealthier (Thurow 1980) to redistribute income.

Although plausible, especially in terms of the expansion of government associated with the Great Society programs of the Johnson administration, this explanation has been only weakly developed. Aside from the inherent difficulties of operationalizing and measuring the concepts implicit in the interpretation, the precise role of relative deprivation and altruism in redistributive policy is only poorly understood.

We formalize this explanation of the expansion of the public sector in the following manner:

$$SIZE_t = A + B_1 COMMUN_{t-1} \qquad\qquad (3.12)$$

where **COMMUN** indicates the level of societal communication about the level of regional and income inequality in the nation. The level of communication would be expected to be positively related to the size of the government.

ASSESSING THE EXPLANATIONS

These various explanations of the government growth process represent the extant body of knowledge and speculation about government growth that we empirically test in Chapter 4 and draw on to develop an alternative explanation in Part III. For ease of reference, the theoretical specifications of all of the models reviewed are summarized in Table 3.1.

Although more will be said about these models later, several general observations about the existing literature should be offered at this point. The first set of observations concerns the quality of the empirical evidence cited in support of the various explanations of government growth. The second set relates to theoretical shortcomings of the models. These comments on the empirical support and theoretical foundations are important because they guide the work presented in the remainder of this book.

Empirical Support for the Models

As should be obvious, the range of empirical support for the explanations reviewed is quite varied. In some cases — the bureau information monopoly and demonstration effect explanations, — little or no empirical testing has been done. Some explanations — Wagner's Law, and the electoral competition explanation, — have been subject to extensive testing. But even where empirical testing has been conducted, the comparability of results of tests is often compromised by the use of different cases and/or time periods that make it difficult to evaluate the degree of empirical support provided the explanation. More important, many of the existing empirical tests are inadequate. For instance, many of the purported tests (for example, Buchanan and Tullock 1977) merely note the collinear growth of the factor hypothesized to be associated with government growth and the size of government, without attempting to more rigorously assess the cause and effect relationship. To some degree, the same criticisms can be leveled against almost any body of empirical research. However, there are additional problems that are so severe in the study of government growth that they deserve special attention.

Especially troubling, given their superficial rigor, is the dominance of cross-sectional tests of the explanations in the literature. In such tests, the various explanations are examined by comparing government growth rates across several nations (for example, Cameron 1978), states (for example, Fisher 1964; Hansen 1983), or cities (Wagner 1976; Pommerehne and Schneider 1978). Unfortunately, cross-sectional analyses may tell us something about differences across jurisdictions, but they are inadequate for assessing inherently dynamic processes within a single jurisdiction like government growth (Gray 1976; Hofferbert 1981).

And even more important, the various explanations have been tested against each other only rarely. Indeed, Cameron's (1978) cross-national test is the only empirical analysis to competitively test more than two of the extant explanations. Given that these many explanations are attempting to explain the same phenomenon, such competitive testing would seem to be essential, not just a luxury.

As a result of these difficulties, it is impossible, at this stage, to rule out any of the various explanations as a plausible or valid interpretation of the process of government growth. Therefore, we must competitively test the many models using time series analysis over the same time period to facilitate fair comparison of their relative ability to account for expansion of the public sector. We provide such a series of tests in the next chapter.

The Theoretical Base of the Growth Research Program

Although these problems in the empirical evaluation of the several models are serious impediments to assessing their utility in understanding the growth process, even more serious problems are found when the theoretical foundations of the whole government growth research program are examined. In raising these issues here, we are less concerned with the theoretical base of the individual explanations themselves than with how the literature has failed to integrate the many existing explanations of government growth. Although the theoretical rationales of the various models are themselves subject to several criticisms, their collective relationship to the larger enterprise of understanding government growth is an even more severe roadblock to understanding the process of public sector expansion.

As should be obvious at this point, the existing literature consists of a number of simple and separate explanations. Even if they were tested against each other to determine more rigorously which best accounts for government growth, such an enterprise would have limited utility in explaining government growth on two grounds. First, it simply strains credulity to expect that the various explanations are not to some extent additive. The growth of government is a process operative on the most "macro" of scales. To think that we could account for all government expansion by the presence of a crisis, party competition, bureaucratic voting, or any of the other factors cited by the specific explanations stretches reductionist thinking to the extreme. Each may have some effect on the size of government, but it would seem unlikely that any could fully account for the expansion of government. It would seem more reasonable to expect that some combination of the factors from several of the explanations will be necessary to explain the expansion of the public sector.

Second, and more important, all the explanations fail to disaggregate government activity, a failure that is prima facie evidence that none will successfully account for government growth. As seen in Chapter 2, the various components of government activity have expanded or contracted at very different rates. For instance, domestic purchases (in constant dollars) has generally expanded as a share of GDP over the postwar era while the defense purchases share of GDP was decreasing over most of that period. The transfers share has risen and declined at different times. Despite this variety of time trends, the many existing explanations of growth treat the size of government as a single, discrete phenomenon that can be explained by a single factor.

This theoretical failure is most evident in the measures of government size used in the existing empirical tests of the models of growth. Most of the models attempt to explain growth in the scope of government activity. Yet, we have seen that much of the expansion of government's share of the economic pie arises not from the expansion of government activities per se, but from the increasing costs of providing a constant level of activities relative to costs in the private sector. Despite this, most of the tests of these explanations use as their dependent variable a measure of the share of GDP devoted to government in current-dollar terms — and thus undeflated for changes in relative costs. Simple increases in the cost of public goods and services are thereby inevitably confounded with growth in the level of goods and services provided. Although this might be viewed as a simple measurement problem, we believe that it arises from the more general theoretical problem of failure to disaggregate the object of study: the size of government.

These observations combine to suggest that we should begin to integrate the various models by first disaggregating the concept, size of government, and then considering which explanations might reasonably account for each of the components. Before undertaking this step, however, we must provide a sounder empirical foundation for assessing the extant explanations of government growth. In the following chapter, then, we operationalize and competitively test the various models of government growth discussed in this chapter using time series analysis. Following an evaluation of these results, we turn to developing a more complex, but more plausible, explanation of government growth based on disaggregated measures of the size of government.

NOTES

1. For most of the explanations of government growth examined in this book, we believe the causal factors identified have a delayed, as opposed to an immediate, effect on public sector size. For this reason, most independent variables in our formal specifications are "lagged" one year behind the dependent variable, $SIZE_t$.

2. The most plausible version of the electoral competition explanation suggests that a high level of interparty competition and the presence of an election should lead to an increase in the size of government but that a total lack of competition should result in no change (rather than a decrease) in public sector size. Thus, we include $SIZE_{t-1}$ as an independent variable in equation 3.4 with the prediction that its coefficient equals one.

3. Other scholars — pluralist theorists (for example, Dahl 1961, Polsby 1963) — have viewed interest group influence more favorably, arguing that influence is widely dispersed among numerous groups in society. From this point of view, interest group activity can be viewed as healthy for the political process; it is one of the ways in which citizens can express strong preferences about public policy choices. In this sense, it would be possible to conceive of the interest group explanation as a responsive government interpretation of public sector expansion. But we have chosen to treat the explanation as excessive, as most of the theoretical support for it within the government growth literature has viewed group influence as pernicious, rather than healthy.

TABLE 3.1
Summary of the Formal Specifications of the Explanations of Government Growth

Explanation	Equation	Theoretical Specification	Predictions

EXCESSIVE GOVERNMENT EXPLANATIONS

Explanation	Equation	Theoretical Specification	Predictions
Bureau Voting	3.1	$SIZE_t = A + B_1\ GOVEM_{t-1}$, where GOVEM is the size of the public employee voting block	$B_1 > 0$
Fiscal Illusion	3.2	$SIZE_t = A + B_1\ ILLUSION_{t-1}$, where ILLUSION is the degree of illusion evidenced in revenue collection mechanisms	$B_1 > 0$
Bureau Information Monopoly	3.3	$SIZE_t = A + B_1\ MONOP_{t-1}$, where MONOP is the degree to which information is controlled by government bureaus	$B_1 > 0$
Electoral Competition	3.4	$SIZE_t = A + B_1\ SIZE_{t-1} + B_2\ ELECT_t$ $+ B_3\ COMP_{t-1} + B_4\ [(ELECT_t)(COMP_{t-1})]$, where $ELECT_t$ equals 1 if an election is held in year t and 0 otherwise, and COMP is the level of interparty competition	$B_1 = 1$; $B_2 > 0$; $B_3 > 0$; $B_4 > 0$
Interest Group	3.5	$SIZE_t = A + B_1\ INTEREST_{t-1}$, where INTEREST is the strength of interest groups desiring particularized public spending	$B_1 > 0$
Institutional Centralization	3.6	$SIZE_t = a + B_1\ DECENT_{t-1}$, where DECENT is the level of fiscal decentralization of the governmental system	$B_1 > 0$

Table 3.1, Continued

RESPONSIVE GOVERNMENT EXPLANATIONS

Wagner's Law	3.7	$SIZE_t = A + B_1 INCOME_{t-1} + B_2 INTERDEP_{t-1}$ $+ B_3 INDUS_{t-1}$, where INCOME is total personal income, INTERDEP is the level of societal interdependencies, and INDUS is the level of industrialization	$B_1 > 0$; $B_2 > 0$; $B_3 > 0$
International	3.8	$SIZE_t = A + B_1 TRADE_{t-1}$, where TRADE is the level of dependence on international trade	$B_1 > 0$
Supply-Side	3.9	$SIZE_t = A + B_1 TAXABLE_{t-1}$, where TAXABLE is the extent to which the organization of economic activity renders income easily taxable	$B_1 > 0$
Party Control	3.10	$SIZE_t = A + B_1 PARTY_{t-1}$, where PARTY is the degree of liberal party control of the government	$B_1 > 0$
Concentration-Displacement	3.11	$SIZE_t = A + B_1 SIZE_{t-1} + B_2 CRISIS_t$, where CRISIS equals 0 in the absence of crisis and a value greater than 0 when a crisis exists	$B_1 = 1$; $B_2 > 0$
Demonstration Effect	3.12	$SIZE_t = A + B_1 COMMUN_{t-1}$, where COMMUN is level of societal communication about the level of regional and income inequality	$B_1 > 0$

Source: Compiled by the authors.

4

TESTING THE
EXPLANATIONS

INTRODUCTION

The single-factor explanations of government growth reviewed in Chapter 3 collectively represent the social sciences' understanding of the phenomenon of public sector expansion. But these explanations indicate the tendency in the literature to attempt to explain all government growth using a single independent variable. We argued in Chapter 3 that such an effort is unrealistic. First, different components of government activity have expanded (or contracted) at quite different rates and are likely governed by different change processes. Thus, different explanations probably must be developed for the various components. Furthermore, even growth in individual components of government activity are unlikely to be explained with a single-factor explanation. The change processes of government are too complex to be modeled so simply. We will address these theoretical shortcomings when we develop our theory of government growth in Part III.

A more immediate concern is that despite the theoretical shortcomings of the various single-factor explanations, substantial empirical support has been cited for several of these models. Such empirical support should not be easily dismissed without a clear demonstration of why that support was obtained. Quite simply, we have a responsibility to show why some of these models appear to work so well and to demonstrate why such evidence should not be accepted on its face. Most important in this regard is the use of inappropriate measures of the size of government. As discussed in the previous two chapters, most of the explanations of government growth attempt to account for real increases in the scope of government activity relative to total economic activity. But empirical tests of these explanations generally employ measures of the size of government that confound such real increases in scope with simple increases in the cost of public sector goods and services relative to those in the private sector. In this chapter, we demonstrate that much of the empirical support previously garnered for the existing models of government growth is an artifact of this mismeasurement of the real size of government.

A second purpose for testing the single-factor explanations is to develop some preliminary evidence to assist in the theory-building endeavor of Part III. The various explanations have only been tested in isolation of each other and with widely varied methods. Our testing of all the models over the same time period using the same method of analysis will allow for a more complete description of the empirical support available for each of the explanations developed previously in the literature. Obviously, evidence that one of the simple models provides a somewhat better empirical account of the growth process than others is not in and of itself sufficient grounds for including or excluding a given factor from consideration in the models in Chapter 5. Still, in conjunction with theoretical support, such empirical evidence can help inform such model building.

The empirical assessment of the existing explanations of the government growth process is undertaken in three steps. First, we will operationalize the existing models and test them over the same time period employing the dependent variable used in most previous empirical tests: the size of government relative to GDP measured in current dollars. Such tests will allow us to competitively assess the explanatory ability of the several models on their own ground. We then repeat these same tests using a more appropriate indicator of the dependent variable measured in constant dollars. This is a measure that does not confound increases in the scope of government activity with simple changes in the relative costs of public and private sector goods and services. Finally, we will compare and contrast the results of these two sets of tests to assess the empirical limits of the existing explanations of the process of government growth.

TESTING THE EXPLANATIONS WITH CURRENT-DOLLAR MEASURES

In this section, we operationalize and test all but one of the explanations of government growth presented in the last chapter using current-dollar measures of the size of government. We do not test the bureau information monopoly model because we are unable to measure the factor it presumes to drive government expansion: the degree to which government bureaus control information.

Operationalizing the Models in Current-Dollar Terms

The same dependent variable is employed in the tests of all the explanations. The size of the public sector in year t ($SIZE_t$) is measured with the current-dollar indicator standard in the literature: the ratio of total government expenditures in year t to GDP in the same year. This measure will be denoted $size_t^n$. [Several notational rules established with this measure will be preserved throughout the book. In contrast to the variable names for concepts (which are in capital letters), the variable names for empirical indicators will be in lowercase letters. The current-dollar measure of size has the superscript "n" (for nominal); the constant-dollar measure will be designated with the superscript "r" (for real).]

The primary data source used to measure this and most of the other variables is CITIBASE. The sources for the few measures not constructed using CITIBASE data are cited in Table 4.1. Annual data for nearly all indicators used in the tests were collected for the period, 1948 to 1982 (some exceptions are described below). Although we will discuss our operationalizations of the independent variables for each of the explanations to be tested, we have summarized the indicators on the left half of Table 4.1.

The first model to be tested, the bureau voting explanation, suggests that the share of economic activity devoted to the public sector rises as the voting power of public employees increases. As we have seen, the level of bureaucratic voting power is usually conceptualized in terms of the size of the bureau voting block relative to the size of the electorate as a whole. Thus, the variable **govem** is measured by the ratio of the number of full- or part-time public employees to the size of the population having reached the age of 20 years or more.[1] Given this indicator, the bureau voting explanation (equation 3.1) is operationalized by

$$\text{size}_t = a + b_1 \text{ govem}_{t-1} + e_t \tag{4.1}$$

where b_1 should be positive.

Operationalizing the concepts underlying the fiscal illusion explanation is more difficult because of the many forms of illusionary fiscal structures identified in the literature (Goetz 1977). Indeed, nearly every revenue source has been identified as illusionary in some way (Lowery 1985). Nevertheless, three sources of fiscal illusion are most commonly cited in presentations of this explanation; each justifies a specific indicator we develop.

The first source of illusion is tax withholding. Public finance scholars have long argued that tax payments made by government withholding from wages leads taxpayers to underestimate their actual tax burdens relative to what they would have estimated those burdens to be under more direct forms of revenue collection (Enrick 1964; Wagstaff 1965). In the United States, the revenue sources that have most heavily relied on withholding collection procedures are the income tax and social insurance taxes. Therefore, one independent variable used to test the fiscal illusion explanation is **wheld** — the proportion of total state, local, and federal receipts (excluding grants-in-aid) raised by federal, state, and local income taxes and social insurance taxes.

The second source of illusion is reliance on deficit financing. As Buchanan and Wagner (1977), Vickrey (1961), and others have conceptualized this source of fiscal illusion, deficit financing leads citizens to underestimate the true long-term costs of current public sector expenditures, thereby encouraging them to demand more than an optimal supply of public goods and services. Thus, we use the variable, **debt**, the ratio of federal, state, and local government debt to federal, state, and local government expenditures. Higher values of this ratio are assumed to reflect a greater degree of fiscal illusion than lower levels of reliance on debt.

The third source of illusion commonly cited is revenue complexity. Highly complex tax systems — those that rely on a large number of small taxes rather than a few larger revenue extraction devices — are hypothesized to lead citizens to underestimate their total tax burdens (Craig and Heins 1980). Such underestimation, again, is expected to lead taxpayers to demand more public goods and services than they would if the full costs of those goods and services were known. This source of illusion is measured by **complex**, an inverse-scored Herfindahl Index of Revenue Concentration (see Wagner 1976, p. 55). The index was constructed with data on federal, state, and local government reliance on eight forms of taxation: corporate profits taxes, business nontax revenue, customs revenue, estate-gift tax revenue, excise tax revenue, income tax revenue, social insurance contributions, and indirect business tax revenue. A higher value on the index indicates a higher degree of dispersion of the revenue collection function across the eight forms of taxation and, therefore, greater tax system complexity.

Unfortunately, data were not available for the full time period for **wheld** and **complex**. Therefore, this particular model is tested using data for a somewhat shorter time series, covering the period 1959 to 1982. In particular, the model tested is

$$\text{size}_t = a + b_1\text{wheld}_{t-1} + b_2\text{debt}_{t-1} + b_3\text{complex}_{t-1} + e_t \tag{4.2}$$

where all slope coefficients are expected to be greater than zero.

The third model to be tested addresses the role of electoral competition. This explanation suggests that high levels of competition and the occurrence of elections are associated with increased spending as elected officials attempt to secure an electoral advantage through budget growth. Moreover, this explanation suggests interaction between level of interparty competition (**COMP**) and the presence of elections (**ELECT**) in influencing the size of government as reflected in equation 3.4.

The level of party competition is measured by an index (**comp**) defined in Table 4.1 and ranging in value from zero to one. The index would equal zero if a single party controlled the presidency and all seats in both houses of Congress. It would equal one — among other situations — if the Democrats controlled all seats in the Senate and House but the president was Republican. Separate dichotomous measures for presidential and off-year congressional elections are included in the model; **presel** equals 1 in a year of a presidential election and 0 otherwise, and **offel** only equals 1 in years of congressional, but no presidential, elections. The inclusion of two election variables necessitates two multiplicative terms in the model to be estimated, [comp_{t-1}) (**presel**$_t$)] and [(comp_{t-1}) (**offel**$_t$)]. The two election dummies, **presel** and **offel**, are not temporally lagged relative to the dependent variable as the competition measure is because, if elections do lead officials to expand the size of government, they should undertake such expansion so that it occurs in the year of the election (for maximum electoral advantage). Thus, in operational form, the electoral competition explanation is[2]

$$size_t = a + b_1 size_{t-1} + b_2 comp_{t-1} + b_3 presel_t + b_4 offel_t$$
$$+ b_5[(comp_{t-1})(presel_t)] + b_6[(comp_{t-1})(offel_t)] + e_t \qquad (4.4)$$

where all slope coefficients are expected to be positive and b_1 equals one.

The remaining complication that needs to be addressed is the operationalization of the lagged value of the dependent variable, **size**, that appears as an independent variable in equation 4.4. When there is first order autocorrelation in a time series regression equation (that is, the correlation between e_t and e_{t-1} is nonzero), the dependent variable lagged one time period will necessarily be correlated with the error term in the equation (Berry 1984, Appendix 1), and it is inappropriate to include the lagged value as an independent variable. This is the case with equation 4.4. Consequently, an instrumental variable is constructed to serve as the indicator, **size**$_{t-1}$. The instrument is constructed with a first-stage regression of **size**$_t$ on a set of variables relating to the factors serving as independent variables in the electoral competition and concentration-displacement explanations (see Table 4.1), the two explanations that include **size**$_{t-1}$ as an independent variable.

Measuring the strength of interest groups demanding greater public spending, the key variable underlying the interest group explanation, is difficult for two reasons. First, what interest group strength entails is not intuitively obvious. However, many treatments of this explanation stress the voting power of population subgroups, a conceptualization that suggests that the size of the group as a voting block is an appropriate way to assess strength. This, however, raises a second problem. Specifically, we need to avoid the use of enumerations of governmentally defined transfer recipients as our measure of interest group size because such a measure would render this explanation nearly tautological; in a sense, that large groups receive particularized public benefits means that these groups have sufficient power to demand benefits. Accordingly, we have attempted to develop measures of the size of several groups, albeit those that do in fact receive substantial transfer payments, where the definition of the group is not explicitly based on the reception of benefits. Although imperfect, such measures avoid the most obvious form of the tautology risk. To be more precise, we employ measures of the voting block size of four groups, each of which is reputed to hold significant interest group voting power: the elderly (**old:vote**), veterans (**vet:vote**), farmers (**farm:vote**), and the poor (**poor:vote**). The size of each group is measured as a proportion of the voting age population.[3] The resulting equation is

$$\text{size}_t = a + b_1\text{old:vote}_{t-1} + b_2\text{farm:vote}_{t-1} + b_3\text{vet:vote}_{t-1}$$
$$+ \ b_4\text{poor:vote}_{t-1} + e_t \qquad (4.5)$$

where all slope coefficients are expected to be positive.

The institutional centralization explanation leads us to expect that lower levels of fiscal decentralization are associated with a greater ability by government to resist pressures to expand the size of the public sector. We measure two aspects of the level of decentralization, **DECENT**, in equation 3.6. The first of these, **revcen**, is the ratio of federal government receipts to total federal, state, and local receipts, excluding grants-in-aid. The degree of reliance on central government finance is inversely related to **DECENT**. A second aspect of fiscal centralization is also introduced into the model given the extensive controversy in the literature on the spending effects of intergovernmental aid (Anton 1983). Some have argued that the use of intergovernmental aid increases overall spending by reducing the need of the recipient level of government to confront fully the tax costs of its spending decisions. Reliance on intergovernmental aid is measured by **aid**, the ratio of federal and state grants-in-aid to total federal, state, and local expenditures. Thus, the model to be tested is

$$\text{size}_t = a + b_1\text{revcen}_{t-1} + b_2\text{aid}_{t-1} + e_t \qquad (4.6)$$

where b_1 is expected to be negative, and b_2 is hypothesized to be positive.

Wagner's Law specifies three distinct ways in which growing industrialization is expected to be associated with the expansion of the public sector. The first, the income elasticity effect, is the easiest to assess, as the variable **INCOME** in equation 3.7 can be measured quite directly. The indicator, total U.S. personal income, will be denoted **income**.

The second component of Wagner's Law pertaining to increased societal interdependencies accompanying industrialization is much more difficult to operationalize. The most frequently used indicator for level of societal interdependencies is the percentage of population living in urban areas (Mann 1980; Borcherding 1977b). But adequate time series data for urban population is not available. Thus we must rely on a less direct surrogate. Our approach is guided by considerations of the debate over social expenditures, especially transfers, which have increased rapidly in the postwar era. We expect the role of increasing social interdependencies in the United States during this period to be reflected primarily in demands for greater social expenditures for subgroups of the population, the needs of whom were formerly met via nongovernmental forms of service provision. Two such groups are the young and the old. The size of both subpopulations tends to increase in industrialized societies at the same time as the institutions that formerly met their service needs — extended families, charities, child labor — decline in relative importance. Thus, the size of the highly service-dependent population is included as an independent variable — measured by **depend**, the percentage of the population less than 18 or greater than 64 years old.

The third component of Wagner's Law refers to the increasing investment needs of industry as societies become more industrialized. The indicator for level of industrialization is predicated on a recognition that industrialization is reflected by a rising share of the economy involved in manufacturing. Thus we follow the choice of Mann (1980) and measure the level of industrialization with **indus**, the proportion of GNP generated in the manufacturing sector. Hence our final specification includes three independent variables:

$$\text{size}_t = a + b_1 \text{income}_{t-1} + b_2 \text{depend}_{t-1} + b_3 \text{indus}_{t-1} + e_t \qquad (4.7)$$

Each slope coefficient is expected to be positive.

The international explanation hypothesizes that the level of an economy's reliance on international trade is positively related to the size of the public sector. Accordingly, we employ two measures of international trade, one to reflect each of its two forms. **Exp** is the ratio of total exports of goods and services to GDP while **imp** denotes the ratio of total imports to GDP. Consequently, the operational version of the international explanation (equation 3.8) is

$$\text{size}_t = a + b_1 \text{exp}_{t-1} + b_2 \text{imp}_{t-1} + e_t \qquad (4.8)$$

where both b_1 and b_2 are predicted to be greater than zero.

In their presentation of the supply-side explanation, Kau and Rubin (1981) point to three specific changes in the composition of the labor force that they hypothesize are associated with greater ease of collecting revenue and, thus, a larger public sector: increases in the level of female participation in the labor force and decreases in the levels of self-employment and farm employment. We include measures of each of these in our test equation. Specifically, **selfem** is the percentage of the labor force that is self-employed, **farmem** is the proportion of the working age population engaged in full- or part-time farm employment, and **femlab** is the size of the female labor force as a percentage of working age female population. In the latter two indicators, the working age population is assumed to be those 20 years and older. As such, our test version of the supply-side explanation is

$$\text{size}_t = a + b_1\text{selfem}_{t-1} + b_2\text{farmem}_{t-1} + b_3\text{femlab}_{t-1} + e_t \qquad (4.9)$$

The coefficients for **selfem** and **farmem** are expected to be negative; b_3 should be positive.

The party control explanation leads to a belief that the size of government rises and falls with the electoral fortunes of political parties representing distinct views on the appropriate role of government in society. Conservative control is expected to be associated with less government while liberal party control should lead to more government provision of goods and services. We assess this explanation with the measure **party**, an index ranging from 0 to 1, with higher numbers associated with more extensive liberal party control. The index is designed to give equal weight to control of the national government and to control of the 50 state governments. In constructing this measure, we assume that Democratic national office holders and nonsouthern Democratic governors are from a liberal party, and that Republicans and southern Democratic governors are from a conservative party. So, for example, a **party** score of 0 indicates complete Republican party control of the executive and legislative branches of the federal government and of the governorship of all nonsouthern states (see Table 4.1 for a detailed definition of **party**). The resulting equation is

$$\text{size}_t = a + b_1\text{party}_{t-1} + e_t \qquad (4.10)$$

where b_1 is expected to be positive.

The concentration-displacement explanation emphasizes the role of crises in increasing the share of the economy devoted to the public sector. Crises are expected to alter the public's expectations about the appropriate size of government so that the public sector grows in a ratchetlike manner. To operationalize the lagged value of the dependent variable in this explanation (equation 3.11), we use the same indicator, $size_{t-1}$, constructed for the electoral competition explanation. Measuring the existence of (and severity of) crisis conditions is more difficult. Clearly, major depressions and wars constitute national crises. But none of the postwar recessions seem severe enough to be viewed as crises. Therefore, we must limit crises to wars in our analysis. Since a "war/no war" dummy variable would fail to distinguish crises based on severity, we have chosen the indicator, number of combat deaths (to be denoted **deaths**), to measure **CRISIS**. These indicators result in the model

$$size_t = a + b_1 size_{t-1} + b_2 deaths_t + e_t \qquad (4.11)$$

where b_2 should be positive and b_1 equals one.

The final explanation, the demonstration effect interpretation, points to the role of increasing societal communication in spurring growth in the public sector. Tarschys' presentation of this model stresses the role of mass communication in publicizing inequities and thereby encouraging transfer expenditure altruism on the part of the wealthy. Alternatively, Jennings (1980) points to the role of urban riots in informing the public about inequities. We employ indicators to tap both these sources of communication. Specifically, **mass** is the proportion of households with television sets and is used to represent the general level of mass communication. Alternatively, **riots** indicates the number of urban disturbances occurring in a given year. The formalized model is

$$size_t = a + b_1 mass_{t-1} + b_2 riots_{t-1} + e_t \qquad (4.12)$$

where it is predicted that both b_1 and b_2 are positive.

Current-Dollar Test Results

The coefficients of the 11 models were initially estimated using ordinary least squares (OLS) regression analysis. Only in the case of the fiscal illusion explanation (equation 4.2) did the Durbin-Watson statistic rule out significant autocorrelation. The remaining equations were reestimated using pseudo-GLS, a technique appropriate when autocorrelation is present (Hibbs 1974).·[4]

The results of the tests of the various explanations are presented in Table 4.2. In general, the majority of models work well when a current-dollar measure of the size of government is employed. The results appear to provide relatively strong support for many of the explanations of government growth developed in the previous literature. First, we review the empirical results for the excessive government explanations.

The bureau voting model (equation 4.1) results, for example, seem to provide strong support for the notion that the size of the bureaucratic voting block is positively associated with the nominal size of government. The positive coefficient estimate for **govem**, the measure of the number of public employees relative to the size of the voting population is significant at the .001 level and the R-square value for the equation is quite high: .46.

Supportive results were also found for the institutional centralization model (equation 4.6), where one of the measures of decentralization, **aid**, produces a positive and highly significant coefficient estimate ($p <$ .001). As expected, greater intergovernmental aid appears to be associated with a larger public sector. Also consistent with the logic of this explanation, the estimate for the measure of revenue decentralization, **revcen**, is negative, albeit nonsignificant. Still, both coefficients carry the expected sign, and the model is able to account for much of the variance in the current-dollar measure of size of government as the R-square value is .73.

Several of the coefficients in the fiscal illusion model (equation 4.2) have the expected positive sign and are significant at the .05 level or better. Specifically, the measures of reliance on withheld taxes and debt financing generated the predicted results. Contrary to expectations, however, the coefficient estimate for the measure of tax system complexity (**complex**) is negative and significant, indicating that reliance on a more complex array of revenue tools is associated with a smaller public sector. Despite this, the R-square value of this equation is very high: .91. Although the results are somewhat mixed, they apparently provide substantial support for the illusion interpretation of government growth.

Less supportive results were found for the electoral competition model (equation 4.4). Specifically, as seen in Table 4.2, the R-square value for this model is quite low relative to those just examined —

only .17. Moreover, two of the five coefficient estimates carry the wrong sign: those for the off-year election dummy variable (offel) and the multiplicative term involving presel and comp. Moreover, none of the correctly signed coefficients come close to being statistically significant at the usual criterion levels. In sum, these results provide little support for the electoral competition explanation.

The weakest results were found for the interest group model. Table 4.2 shows that the coefficients for three of the four measures of the size of interest groups — those for farmers, veterans, and the poor — are negative in sign, indicating that the size of government seems to decline as these groups become larger. Moreover, the estimates for the last two of these variables are statistically significant at the .05 level. Only the indicator of the size of the elderly population (old:vote) produces the expected positive coefficient, and it is not statistically significant. In short, the results provide little support for the interest group explanation of the expansion of the public sector.

We also find support for several of the responsive government explanations using our nominal measure of the size of government. Specifically, two of the three variables included in the test of Wagner's Law (equation 4.7) produce coefficients of the expected sign that are highly significant. The variables designed to tap the income elasticity (income) and interdependency (depend) components of the law work as Wagner's analysis would lead us to expect. Contrary to expectations, the coefficient estimate for the indicator employed to assess the infrastructure demands of industrialization (indus) is negative, but this coefficient is very weak in magnitude. Moreover, the Wagner's Law equation produces a healthy R-square value of .81. In short, Wagner's Law seems to work when a current-dollar measure of the size of government is employed.

Similarly, the test of the international explanation (equation 4.8) produces results that are apparently supportive of that explanation's account of government growth. Both the export (exp) and import (imp) reliance measures are positive as expected (though only the latter was significant at the .05 level), indicating that government seems to grow as reliance on international trade increases. The R-square value of this equation, although not of the same magnitude as that observed for some of the others, is sizable: .47.

The current-dollar test yields supportive results for the demonstration effect model (equation 4.12), too. Both of the estimated coefficients, those for mass and riots, are positive as this explanation would lead us to expect. Moreover, the coefficient for the measure of the level of mass communications is significant at the .01 level. The R-square value (.34) for this model, however, is somewhat lower than those observed for several of the other models with supportive results.

Mixed, but generally supportive findings are produced for the supply-side model (equation 4.9), with two of the three estimated coefficients carrying the expected sign. More precisely, the coefficient for **selfem**, the measure of the size of the self-employed population, was negative as expected, and the coefficient for **femlab**, the measure of the rate of female labor force participation, was positive. Only the latter was statistically significant. The coefficient for the indicator of farm employment, **farmem**, is positive (instead of negative as expected) but is very weak in magnitude. Moreover, this equation produced the highest R-square value of any of the current-dollar tests, exceeding the .90 level.

The remaining two responsive government explanations did not fare as well in the current-dollar tests. For the party control model, the estimated coefficient of the degree of liberal party control was virtually zero; the bivariate model produced an R-square value of .01. The results for the test of the concentration-displacement explanation (equation 4.11) are unsupportive as well. The sign of the measure of the level of military conflict, **deaths**, generates the wrong sign, and the coefficient for **size$_{t-1}$** is substantially less than the predicted value of 1.0.

In sum, the tests using a current-dollar measure of public sector size provide support for most of the explanations of government growth. Moreover, the results suggest that elements of both the responsive and excessive interpretations of government growth may be correct. Indeed, if current-dollar measures were an appropriate way to measure the focus of these explanations — growth in the scale and scope of government activity — we could seek to integrate several of these explanations into a more comprehensive account of the growth process. Unfortunately, a current-dollar measure is invalid; as we have reiterated several times, it seriously confounds real growth of government activity and cost growth. To more validly assess these explanations, then, we must turn to tests of the models employing constant-dollar measures of the size of the public sector.

Operationalizing the Models in Constant-Dollar Terms

In testing the models of government growth, our goal is to restrict the number of changes to only those associated with the measurement of real, as opposed to nominal, values of variables. Thus, the same 1948 to 1982 time period is employed, and all of the same basic measures are used (see the right half of Table 4.1). The only differences between the tests to be presented and those just examined lie in the deflation of some of the measures to reflect the real values of concepts. The implicit price deflators (IPDs) presented in this section, like most of the data used in these analyses, were gathered from CITIBASE. All the real measures are constructed with a 1972 base year.

The most important of the reoperationalizations concerns the dependent variable: the size of government. As with the previous tests, we again start with the ratio of total government expenditures to GDP. In this case, however, the numerator and denominator of the ratio are adjusted with implicit price deflators. Specifically, as seen in Table 4.1, government expenditures were deflated by the IPD for government expenditures, and GDP was deflated with the IPD for GDP.

We also deflated a number of the independent variables employed in the previous tests. For example, the total personal income measure in the Wagner's Law equation (4.7), **income**, was deflated with the IPD for national income; the indicator of the level of industrialization (**indus**) was also deflated, in this case, with the IPDs for manufacturing and GNP applied to the respective components of the ratio. Similarly, the import (**imp**) and export (**exp**) measures in the international model (equation 4.8) were deflated with IPDs for imports and exports, respectively. The indicators of all other independent variables already reflect real values and, therefore, did not have to be deflated for the new tests.

Constant-Dollar Test Results

The models were reestimated with the revised measures using OLS regression. Analysis of partial autocorrelation coefficients and correlograms indicated that the assumption of a lack of autocorrelation was violated for a number of models. Therefore, these models were reestimated using pseudo-GLS. The order of their respective autoregressive structures are reported in Table 4.3.

The results for the constant-dollar tests of the government growth models are presented in Table 4.3. As can be seen, the bureau voting explanation (equation 4.1) fares quite poorly when tested using a real-dollar measure of the size of government. Specifically, the estimated coefficient for **govem** is now opposite to both what was observed in the current-dollar test of the model and the expectation of the model. The coefficient is now negative and significant at the .001 level, and the equation produces an R-square value of .62. In real terms, then, the size of the bureau voting block is negatively associated with public sector size.

Similarly, the estimated coefficients for the fiscal illusion model (equation 4.2) in the revised test provide little support for that explanation. Contrary to expectations, the coefficients for **wheld** and **debt** are negative, and the former is significant at the .05 level. Only the reestimated coefficient for **complex**, the measure of tax system complexity, is consistent with the prediction of the fiscal illusion explanation.

The weak results observed for the current-dollar test of the electoral competition explanation (equation 4.4) remain essentially unchanged in the results presented in Table 4.3. All but one of the estimated coefficients retain the same sign as that observed previously; three of the six carry the sign opposite to that hypothesized. And again, none of the coefficients are significantly different from zero (except that for the lagged value of **size**).

In one of the few cases where the use of constant-dollar measures actually serves to improve the support for an explanation, the new results for the interest group model (equation 4.5) exhibit two positive coefficients as expected, those for **old:vote** and **farm:vote**. This level of support, however, is hardly strong. The coefficients of the other two variables retained their negative signs, and neither of the two correctly signed coefficients was statistically significant.[5]

In the current-dollar test, strong support was found for the institutional centralization model (equation 4.6), with both coefficients carrying the expected sign. However, the signs for both **revcen** and **aid** reverse when constant-dollar measures are employed. When the more valid measure of government size is used, greater fiscal centralization is associated with a larger-sized government, while reliance on intergovernmental aid is negatively related to government size, with the former relationship significant at the .001 level. Taken as a set, then, the excessive government explanations receive virtually no support when tested properly using real-dollar measures for variables.

But much the same result occurs with the responsive government explanations. This is especially evident in the revised test of Wagner's Law (equation 4.7). The signs of both coefficients that were in the expected direction and statistically significant in the current-dollar test (**income** and **depend**) reverse. And the negative coefficients for both variables are significant at the .01 level. Only the level of industrialization indicator is now positive as expected, and it is not significant at the usual criterion levels. The supportive results for the international model (equation 4.8) also disappear when deflated measures are used. Contrary to the hypothesis, the coefficient for the imports indicator is now negative and significant at the .01 level. The coefficient for reliance on exports is again positive, but it is not statistically significant.

In the previous test of the supply-side explanation, two of the three estimated coefficients were of the expected sign. However, in the results of the test employing constant-dollar measures, one of these coefficients changes sign. Thus, only the positive coefficient for the level of female labor force participation is consistent with this explanation's predictions, and none of the coefficients are statistically significant.[6]

The results for the party control model (equation 4.10) are equally dismal whether using nominal- or real-dollar measures of the size of government. With constant-dollar measures, the R-square value of the model is only .02. Somewhat more supportive results are found for the concentration-displacement explanation (equation 4.11) in the test using real-dollar measures. Contrary to what we had observed in the previous tests, the estimated coefficient for **deaths** is now positive (but not significant), and the coefficient for $size_{t-1}$ — at .86 — is now fairly close to its predicted value of 1.0. Moreover, the R-square value of the model increases to .32.

Finally, the results for the real-dollar test of the demonstration effect explanation (equation 4.12), like most of those observed to this point, are less supportive of this explanation than those produced when current-dollar measures are employed. Specifically, the formerly positive and significant coefficient for **mass** is now negative and significant. The coefficient for **riots** remains positive but is extremely weak. Also, the use of real-dollar measures reduces the R-square value of the model to .24.

In conclusion, the use of a more valid real-dollar measure of the size of government strikingly alters the degree of confirmatory support provided the various explanations of government growth. To summarize the differences in results between the current- and constant-dollar tests, Table 4.4 presents both the expected signs of the coefficients of the models and those actually observed in the two sets of tests. One crude indicator of the dramatic extent to which the results vary across the two tests is to note that 12 coefficients are statistically significant ($p < .05$) in the set of current-dollar tests, and that 9 of the 12 switch signs with the constant-dollar tests. Quite clearly, the measurement issue is an important one. It matters a great deal whether real- or current-dollar measures are used. But what does all of this say about our knowledge of the government growth process? We now turn to this issue.

EVALUATING THE RESULTS OF THE TESTS

In this chapter, we have attempted to confront the many explanations of government growth with data in a manner that allows us to directly compare and assess their relative explanatory power. At the same time, we have tried to assess the degree to which the use of the traditional measure of the size of government undercuts the empirical support found in the literature for these explanations.

In terms of the first consideration, although degree of support varies across explanations, the tests employing current-dollar measures indicate that most of the models are valid to at least some degree.[7] Indeed, this is consistent with the pattern of empirical support for the various explanations in the literature. If the current-dollar tests are considered appropriate, then it becomes difficult — at least on empirical grounds alone — to distinguish which explanation or set of explanations best accounts for the growth of government in the postwar era. However, the tests employing a constant-dollar measure of the size of government suggest that such a discrimination may be unnecessary. Simply put, none of the models seem capable of accounting for postwar U.S. government growth when real-dollar measures are employed.

The meaning of our results then depends on how one answers two questions. First, is the use of real-dollar measures appropriate? And second, if their use is appropriate, what should our empirical results tell us about the prospects for adequately explaining the expansion of the public sector?

We believe the use of constant-dollar measures is both appropriate and necessary. And the reasoning behind this answer is very simple. The explanations tested in this chapter attempt to account for real change in the scope of government activity as a function of real changes in an array of hypothesized determinants. Unfortunately, the measures used in previous empirical assessments of these explanations — the current-dollar indicators of the size of government and several of the independent variables as well — confound such changes in real values with changes in their relative costs. These indicators are, therefore, invalid measures of the concepts they purport to measure.

However, it might be argued that our tests of these explanations using more valid indicators, the deflated or constant-dollar measures, are equally inappropriate. For instance, it might be argued that our specifications of the models are inadequate, that relevant variables have been excluded, that linear models may be inappropriate in some cases, and so on. This contention, however, is belied by the apparent success of models in the current-dollar tests. That is, our specifications of the models generate levels of support for the explanations that are similar to those reported in previous research. Thus, if the models are provided so little support by the real-dollar tests, something other than our specifications of the models must account for those poor results.

What lessons, then, do the findings of this chapter offer about explaining government growth in the United States? First and most important, we must resist the temptation to conclude from our empirical analysis that the existing models can tell us little or nothing about the process of government growth.

Although the results provide little support for the existing explanations of government growth as they are usually specified, there is ample reason to believe that those specifications were fundamentally flawed initially. The reasoning behind this argument was presented at the end of the previous chapter in the discussion of the theoretical problems underlying the explanations. Specifically, we noted that the tendency of the explanations to deal with all government activity as an aggregate makes it most unlikely that the extant models will work. In Chapter 2, we showed that different components of government activity have expanded and contracted at different rates; with such varied patterns, no single explanation can be expected to account for the size of government as an aggregate. Furthermore, regardless of the level of aggregation of the dependent variable, any single-factor explanation — like all those tested here — is unlikely to account for a phenomenon as complex as the changing size of government. This does not mean that party control, personal income growth, or increases in government employment are unimportant in understanding why government grows, only that each factor by itself is unlikely to account for the totality of the expansion of the public sector. In any event, given the problems with the explanations, we believe the prior probability that these models would survive direct confrontation with data was quite small.

Additionally, the explanations reviewed in this chapter and the tests with constant-dollar measures leave open the question of what accounts for the largest share of the nominal growth of government in the postwar era: cost growth, that is, growth due to increases in the costs of government relative to those in the private sector. If we are to understand government growth in all its forms, we must develop a model capable of accounting for changes in the relative costs of government goods and services as well as for changes in the scope of government activity.

In short, we believe that the primary message to be derived from the results of the tests using real-dollar measures of public sector size is that we need better theory about why government grows. Such theory must distinguish between growth due to real increases in the level of public sector activity and growth due to the changing relative costs of public and private sector goods and services. It must also develop more precise explanations for growth of different components of overall real expenditures. And it is likely that such a theory will need to employ various elements of some of the existing explanations in a more integrative manner. We present such a theory in the next part of this book.

NOTES

1. We recognize that the minimum voting age for presidential elections varied across the period of analysis from 18 to 21, and that in some years, minimum voting ages for state elections varied from state to state. But the difference resulting from using 18 instead of 21 to define voting age population is negligible for our results. So for convenience, we uniformly assume the voting age population to be 20 years and above for all years of analysis.

2. We have skipped over 4.3 in numbering equations in this chapter to make the numbers of operational form equations in this chapter match those of the theoretical forms in Chapter 3.

3. The indicator **poor:vote** is the number of persons below the poverty line as a percentage of the 20 years or older population. For the period from 1959 to 1983, actual data on the number of persons below the poverty line were available. Data for 1948 to 1958 were estimated by regressing the number of persons below the poverty line on the number of recipients of Aid to Families with Dependent Children (AFDC),

the number receiving unemployment compensation, and the number of recipients of Old Age Assistance (OAA), using post-1959 data. Then, actual data for the independent variables in the pre-1959 period are used along with the coefficient estimates to yield estimates for the dependent variable. Thus our estimation of **poor:vote** values for the 1948-1958 period assumes that the relationship between the number of poor and the numbers of welfare programs recipients has been stable over the postwar period.

4.   Each of these equations exhibited autocorrelation and partial autocorrelation functions suggestive of an autoregressive structure. The orders of the autoregressive processes for the equations are presented in Table 4.2.

5.   The substantial R-square of .78 for this model in conjunction with four statistically insignificant regression coefficients suggests that multicollinearity may be partially responsible for the high standard errors for coefficients. This is confirmed by the fact that three of the four independent variables in the model, when regressed on the remaining independent variables, yield R-square values exceeding .92.

6.   Again, a high R-square coefficient (.78) alongside three statistically insignificant partial slope coefficient estimates is a clue that multicollinearity may be severe. Indeed, each of the models' independent variables, when regressed on the remaining independent variables, produces an R-square value greater than .85.

7.   The only exceptions are the electoral competition, interest group, party control, and concentration-displacement explanations.

TABLE 4.1

Description of Indicators Used to Test the Models of Government Size Using Both Current-Dollar and Constant-Dollar Measures of Variables

Variable	Indicator for Current-Dollar Test	Indicator for Constant-Dollar Test
share$_{t-1}$	Ratio of total federal, state and local government expenditures (excluding grants-in-aid) to GDP	[Ratio of total federal, state and local government expenditures (excluding grants-in-aid) to GDP] multiplied by [ratio of IPD for GDP to IPD for government]

(4.1) Bureau Voting explanation

govem	Number of full- and part-time government employees as a percentage of voting-age (i.e., 20 years or older) population	Same as current-dollar measure

(4.2) Fiscal Illusion explanation

wheld	[Government receipts from social insurance contributions and federal, state, and local income taxes] as a percentage of [total federal, state and local government receipts excluding grants-in aid] (data only available for period 1958 to 1982)	Same as current-dollar measure
debt	[Federal, state and local government expenditures minus federal, state and local receipts] as a percentage of [total federal, state and local government expenditures]	Same as current-dollar measure
complex	Herfindahl Index of Revenue Concentration (see Wagner 1976, p. 55) based on eight revenue sources: corporate profits tax, business nontax revenue, customs revenue, estate-gift tax, excise tax, income tax, social insurance contributions, and indirect business tax (data only available for period 1959 to 1982)	Same as current-dollar measure

85

Table 4.1, Continued

(4.4) Electoral Competition Explanation

$size_{t-1}$ Instrumental variable constructed in first-stage regression of $size_t^n$ on

     Instrumental variable constructed in first-stage regression of $size_t^r$ on same independent variables used with current-dollar measure of $size_{t-1}$.

(a) dichotomous variables measuring the party that controls the Congress and the party that controls the presidency,

(b) variables measuring the percentage of seats in the House and the Senate controlled by the Democratic party,

(c) the indicators offel, presel, comp, and deaths.

comp $1 - (2 \mid (HS/4 + SN/4 + PR/2) - .5 \mid)$, where HS = percentage of seats in House controlled by Democrats, SN = percentage of seats in Senate controlled by Democrats, and PR = 1 if the president is a Democrat and 0 if the president is a Republican

     Same as current-dollar measure

presel   Dichotomous variable that equals 1 in a year of a presidential election and 0 otherwise

     Same as current-dollar measure

offel   Dichotomous variable that equals 1 in an off-year election year and 0 otherwise

     Same as current-dollar measure

(4.5) Interest Group explanation

old:vote   Number of people older than 64 as a percentage of the voting age (i.e., 20 years or older) population

     Same as current-dollar measure

farm:vote   Number of people employed in farming as a percentage of twenty years or older population

     Same as current-dollar measure

vet:vote   Number of veterans as a percentage of twenty years or older population

     Same as current-dollar measure

Table 4.1, Continued

poor:vote	Number of persons below the Poverty Line as a percentage of twenty years or older population. For the 1959-1983 period, actual data on the number below the Poverty Line were used. The pre-1959 numbers were estimated based on a regression of the number of persons below the Poverty Line on the number of AFDC recipients, the number receiving unemployment compensation, and the number of OAA recipients	Same as current-dollar measure

(4.6) Institutional Centralization Explanation

revcen	[Federal government receipts] as a percentage of [total federal, state and local government receipts excluding grants-in-aid]	Same as current-dollar measure
aid	Federal and state grants-in-aid to state and/or local governments as a percentage of total federal, state and local expenditures.	Same as current-dollar measure

(4.7) Wagner's Law

income	Total personal income in billions of dollars	Total personal income in billions of dollars divided by IPD for national income
depend	Percentage of population under age 18 or over age 64	Same as current-dollar measure
indus	Ratio of manufacturing GNP to GNP	[Ratio of manufacturing GNP to GNP] multiplied by [ratio of IPD for manufacturing to IPD for GNP]

(4.8) International Explanation

exp	Ratio of total exports of goods and services to GDP	[Ratio of total exports of goods and services to GDP] multiplied by [ratio of IPD for GDP to IPD for exports]
imp	Ratio of total imports of goods and services to GDP	[Ratio of total imports of goods and services to GDP] multiplied by [ratio of IPD for GDP to IPD for imports]

87

Table 4.1, Continued

(4.9)   Supply-Side Explanation

selfem	Percentage of labor force that is self employed	Same as current-dollar measure
farmem	Number of full- and part-time farm employees as a percentage of working age (i.e., 20 years or older) population	Same as current-dollar measure
femlab	Size of female labor force as a percentage of female population 20 years or older	Same as current-dollar measure

(4.10)   Party Control Explanation

party	$((HS/4 + SN/4 + P/2)/2) + ST/2,$	Same as current-dollar measure
	where HS is the percentage of House seats held by Democrats, SN is the percentage of Senate seats held by Democrats, P is 1 if the President is a Democrat and 0 otherwise, and ST equals the number of nonsouthern Democratic governors divided by the total number of governors	

(4.11)   Concentration/Displacement Explanation

size$_{t-1}$	Same as in electoral competition explanation	Same as current-dollar measure
deaths	Number of combat deaths	Same as current-dollar measure

(4.12)   Demonstration Effect Explanation

mass	Percentage of households with television sets	Same as current-dollar measure
riots	Number of urban riots	Same as current-dollar measure

Note: IPD is an abbreviation for implicit price deflator. All IPDs are fixed at 100 in their base year, 1972.

Source: Compiled by the authors.

TABLE 4.2
Estimates of Coefficients for Equations Specifying the Models of Government Size Using Current-Dollar Measures of Variables

Equation	Explanation	Unstandardized Coefficient Estimates (with Standard Errors in Parentheses)	R^2
4.1	Bureau Voting	$size_t^n = .06 + 1.99^{***} (govem_{t-1})$ $(.38)$	.46
4.2	Fiscal Illusion	$size_t^n = .14 + .0070^{***} (wheld_{t-1})$ $(.0010)$ $+.12^* (debt_{t-1}) - .54^* (complex_{t-1})$ $(.05) \qquad (.24)$	.91
4.4	Electoral Competition	$size_t^n = .19 + .33 (size_{t-1}) + .014 (comp_{t-1})$ $(.18) \qquad (.060)$ $+ .024 (presel_t) - .043 (offel_t)$ $(.037) \qquad (.044)$ $- .043 [(comp_{t-1})(presel_t)] +$ $(.072)$ $+ .097 [(comp_{t-1})(offel_t)]$ $(.092)$	.17
4.5	Interest Group	$size_t^n = .41 + .78 (old:vote_{t-1})$ $(.55)$ $- .35 (farm:vote_{t-1}) - .75^{**} (vet:vote_{t-1})$ $(2.80) \qquad (.25)$ $- .40^* (poor:vote_{t-1})$ $(.19)$	.90
4.6	Institutional Centralization	$size_t^n = .26 - .046 (revcen_{t-1})$ $(.154)$ $+ 1.14^{***} (aid_{t-1})$ $(.27)$	.73
4.7	Wagner's Law	$size_t^n = .03 + .000052^{***} (income_{t-1})$ $(.000011)$ $+ .57^{***} (depend_{t-1}) - .065 (indus_{t-1})$ $(.14) \qquad (.240)$	.81

Table 4.2, Continued

4.8	International	$size_t^n = .21 + .21\ (exp_{t-1})$	.47

$$(.44)$$

$$+\ 1.02^*\ (imp_{t-1})$$
$$(.45)$$

4.9	Supply-Side	$size_t^n = .25 - .75\ (selfem_{t-1}) + 1.20\ (farmem_{t-1})$	.92

$$(.44)\qquad\qquad (2.70)$$

$$+.28^{**}\ (femlab_{t-1})$$
$$(.08)$$

4.10	Party Control	$size_t^n = .30 - .0087\ (party_{t-1})$	.01

$$(.0190)$$

4.11	Concentration-Displacement	$size_t^n = .23 + .22\ (size_{t-1}) - .0019\ (deaths_t)$	.09

$$(.16)\qquad\qquad (.0016)$$

4.12	Demonstration Effect	$size_t^n = .23 + .080^{**}\ (mass_{t-1})$	.34

$$(.023)$$

$$+\ .000046\ (riots_{t-1})$$
$$(.000066)$$

$*p < .05;\ **p < .01;\ ***p < .001.$

Note: All equations are estimated using pseudo-GLS except equation 4.2 for which OLS was used (as the Durbin-Watson statistic indicates a lack of significant autocorrelation). All the remaining equations are assumed to have an error term characterized by an autoregressive process of order 1 except equations 4.5, 4.6, and 4.9 (each of which appears to be autoregressive, order 2).

Source: Compiled by the authors.

TABLE 4.3
Estimates of Coefficients for Equations Specifying the Models of Government Size Using Constant-Dollar Measures of Variables

Equation	Explanation	Unstandardized Coefficient Estimates (with Standard Errors in Parentheses)	R^2
4.1	Bureau Voting	$size^r_t = .59 - 1.91^{***} (govem_{t-1})$ $(.27)$	.62
4.2	Fiscal Illusion	$size^r_t = .31 - .0051^{**} (wheld_{t-1})$ $(.0018)$ $- .15 (debt_{t-1}) + .90^* (complex_{t-1})$ $(.08) \qquad (.42)$	.40
4.4	Electoral Competition	$size^r_t = .05 + .86^{**} (size_{t-1}) + .0067 (comp_{t-1})$ $(.25) \qquad (.0496)$ $- .00066 (presel_t) - .014 (offel_t)$ $(.02122) \qquad (.027)$ $- .0029 [(comp_{t-1})(presel_t)] +$ $(.0404)$ $+ .024 [(comp_{t-1})(offel_t)]$ $(.057)$	.36
4.5	Interest Group	$size^r_t = .29 + .42 (old:vote_{t-1})$ $(.73)$ $+ 7.08 (farm:vote_{t-1}) - .38 (vet:vote_{t-1})$ $(3.60) \qquad (.32)$ $- .094 (poor:vote_{t-1})$ $(.237)$	.78
4.6	Institutional Centralization	$size^r_t = -.06 + .63^{***} (revcen_{t-1})$ $(.09)$ $- .12 (aid_{t-1})$ $(.16)$	.90
4.7	Wagner's Law	$size^r_t = .51 - .000097^{***} (income_{t-1})$ $(.000011)$ $- .44^{**} (depend_{t-1}) + .43 (indus_{t-1})$ $(.14) \qquad (.26)$	.72

Table 4.3, Continued

4.8	International	$size_t^r = .43 + .15\ (exp_{t-1})$ $\qquad\qquad (.12)$ $\qquad - .55^{**}\ (imp_{t-1})$ $\qquad\ \ (.15)$	.52
4.9	Supply-Side	$size_t^r = .20 + .40\ (selfem_{t-1}) + 4.3\ (farmem_{t-1})$ $\qquad\qquad (.64) \qquad\qquad\quad (3.9)$ $\qquad + .13\ (femlab_{t-1})$ $\qquad\ \ (.12)$	.78
4.10	Party Control	$size_t^r = .37 - .019\ (party_{t-1})$ $\qquad\qquad\ (.023)$	.02
4.11	Concentration- Displacement	$size_t^r = .05 + .86^{**}\ (size_{t-1}) + .00093\ (deaths_t)$ $\qquad\qquad (.24) \qquad\qquad\quad (.00131)$	.32
4.12	Demonstration Effect	$size_t^r = .41 - .068^{*}\ (mass_{t-1})$ $\qquad\qquad\ (.025)$ $\qquad + .000011\ (riots_{t-1})$ $\qquad\ (.000068)$	.24

*p < .05; **p < .01; ***p < .001.

Note: All equations are estimated using pseudo-GLS. All estimations assume an autoregressive error structure of order 2 except that of equation 4.12 (order 3).

Source: Compiled by the authors.

TABLE 4.4

Signs of Coefficient Estimates for Independent Variables in Equations Specifying the Models of Government Size: Hypothesized Signs According to Models, Signs Using Current-Dollar Measures of Variables, and Signs Using Constant-Dollar Measures of Variables

Equation	Explanation	Variable	Sign Hypothesized By Model	Current-Dollar Version		Constant-Dollar Version	
4.1	Bureau Voting	$govem_{t-1}$	+	+***	.46	-***	.62
4.2	Fiscal Illusion	$wheld_{t-1}$	+	+***	.91	-*	.40
		$debt_{t-1}$	+	+*		-	
		$complex_{t-1}$	+	-*		+*	
4.4	Electoral Competition	$size_{t-1}$	1.00	.19	.17	.86	.36
		$comp_{t-1}$	+	+		+	
		$presel_t$	+	+		-	
		$offel_t$	+	-		-	
		$(comp_{t-1})(presel_t)$	+	-		-	
		$(comp_{t-1})(offel_t)$	+	+		+	
4.5	Interest Group	$oldpop_{t-1}$	+	+	.90	+	.78
		$farmpop_{t-1}$	+	-**		+	
		$vetpop_{t-1}$	+	-		-	
		$poorpop_{t-1}$	+	-*		-	
4.6	Institutional Centralization	$revcen_{t-1}$	-	-	.73	+***	.90
		aid_{t-1}	+	+***		-	
4.7	Wagner's Law	$income_{t-1}$	+	+***	.81	-***	.72
		$depend_{t-1}$	+	+***		-**	
		$indus_{t-1}$	+	-		+	
4.8	International	exp_{t-1}	+	+	.47	+	.52
		imp_{t-1}	+	+*		-**	
4.9	Supply-Side	$selfem_{t-1}$	-	-	.92	+	.78
		$farmem_{t-1}$	-	+		+	
		$femlab_{t-1}$	+	+**		+	
4.10	Party Control	$party_{t-1}$	+	-	.01	-	.01
4.11	Concentration-Displacement	$size_{t-1}$	1.00	.22	.09	.86	.32
		$deaths_t$	+	-		+	
4.12	Demonstration Effect	$mass_{t-1}$	+	+**	.34	-*	.24
		$riots_{t-1}$	+	+		+	

*p < .05; **p < .01; ***p < .001.

Source: Compiled by the authors.

III

A DISAGGREGATED ANALYSIS OF GOVERNMENT GROWTH

5

GROWTH IN THE
COST OF GOVERNMENT

INTRODUCTION

To this point, we have seen that numerous explanations of government growth can be found in the literature. These many explanations were reviewed in Chapter 3 and tested in Chapter 4 employing both constant- and current-dollar measures of the size of government. The current-dollar test results offer support for most of these explanations, support consistent with many previous studies relying on nominal measures of public sector size. But the more appropriate tests, those using real measures of size, paint an entirely different picture of the empirical validity of the various explanations that dominate the literature. The constant-dollar tests suggest that none of the explanations can account for changes in the size of the U.S. public sector in the postwar era.

Given the critical analysis of the extant explanations presented in Chapter 3, this failure should not be especially surprising. The existing explanations constitute a set of single-factor explanations of the government growth process. Given the vast scope of the phenomenon being explained, the size of government in the postwar era, it is naive to expect any one of these single-factor explanations to work.

Moreover, the existing accounts of public sector growth — in seeking to explain the real size of government — do not address growth that is due to the increasing cost of providing public goods and services relative to costs in the private sector, as distinguished from increases in the scope of the goods and services provided. But as demonstrated in Chapter 2, the bulk of the increase in the nominal size of government over the last four decades is due precisely to cost growth. Consequently, any theory that purports to provide an adequate account of the government growth process will have to explain cost growth.

And finally, even if we set aside the phenomenon of cost growth, in attempting to explain changes in the real size of government, the extant explanations of government growth ignore the possibility that different types of government expenditure may require separate explanations. Indeed, we have seen that the overall postwar trend in the ratio of government expenditures to GDP masks widely varying change patterns for several different components or categories of expenditure. For instance while both real domestic purchases and real transfer payments to individuals have expanded relative to GDP in most years since 1950, real defense purchases have generally decreased. Furthermore, the transfers and domestic purchases trends have hardly been identical. Domestic purchases as a share of GDP grew steadily from 1951 to 1975, except for the few years between 1971 to 1973. But since 1975 the domestic purchases share has been decreasing. The real share of GDP devoted to transfers grew during the 1950s and decreased throughout the first half of the 1960s but increased again over the next decade. Since 1975, the transfers share decreased for four years and then began to increase again in 1979. These observations imply that different explanations are probably needed to explain the scope of government with respect to domestic purchases, defense purchases, and transfers.

But would disaggregation of government activity into several components carry us into a subject different from that of government growth? Observations made about the size of government typically refer to a broader phenomenon than the share of GDP devoted to government transfers, the share devoted to domestic purchases, or the share for defense purchases. In both scholarly inquiry and political debate, government growth is typically viewed as something more than the sum of the changes in the sizes of different components of government activity. Yet, that observed growth paths do vary across categories of government expenditure strongly hints that the popular conception of government size might be more an artifact of several distinct, underlying processes yielding levels of government activity in several domains than the result of a single process that can be isolated for analysis. When we contemplate the widely disparate patterns of change of the several categories of public spending, efforts to explain the overall growth of government begin to resemble the nineteenth century naturalist's attempts to understand the nature of the ether. Attaching a simple label, like government growth, to a large and complex phenomenon really does not take one very far in understanding it. Indeed, the use of overly simple categories of analysis may actually inhibit understanding by directing our attention away from more fruitful questions about the specific elements artfully subsumed under the label. In short, the phenomenon of overall government growth may be more a rhetoric-gilded chimera than something that can be subject to scholarly analysis.

But if disaggregation is considered appropriate, two other issues are raised immediately. How far shall we disaggregate government size? And on what basis? If we disaggregate the size of government in an extreme way — developing share-of-GDP measures for every budget category — then we would essentially be replicating the literature on the determinants of government spending, albeit with a slightly different dependent variable (the expenditure GDP ratio rather than the expenditure itself). Beyond the inherent theoretical confusion this would involve, it would almost surely sever any relationship between our analysis and the topic, government growth. Thus, like the excessive aggregation inherent in the use of global measures of the size of government, extreme disaggregation is unlikely to help us understand anything more about government growth than what we already know from the extensive literature on public spending.

Consequently, if inquiry into the topic of government growth is to avoid the twin pitfalls of excessive aggregation, which would confine us to the fruitless task of seeking to explain what is probably an artifact of several separate and only partially related phenomena, and excessive disaggregation, which would force us to reject completely the view of the forest for chopping down innumerable trees, the size of government must be reconceptualized at some mid-range level. This mid-range level should still leave us in striking distance of the normative and efficiency concerns raised in Chapter 1 but should entail sufficient disaggregation to allow for plausible and theoretically meaningful statements about cause and effect.

Numerous mid-range typologies of public expenditure categories might be employed as the basis of such disaggregation (see Ott and Ott 1969; Borcherding 1977c; Tiegen 1980). However, the typology employed should group government activities into the minimum number of theoretically meaningful components required to account for the overall growth of government. This criterion forces the analyst to disaggregate, but as little as possible in order to preserve the view of the government growth "forest." In the analyses that follow, we develop separate models to account for public sector cost growth, as well as real change, in the shares of GDP allocated toward government transfer payments to individuals, domestic purchases of goods and services, and defense purchases.

The justification for disaggregating government growth into these four categories is both empirical and theoretical. The empirical reason is the widely different trends of the four components in the postwar era. The theoretical reason is a belief that changes in the four categories result from quite different processes. This will become clear when we present our distinct explanations for growth in the four components. The issue of whether further disaggregation is required must be left until we can assess how successful we are in accounting for government growth using our four-element typology. We will return to this issue in the concluding chapter of the book.

In developing our models, we continue to view the responsive and excessive interpretations as distinct frameworks for explaining government growth. Therefore for each of the four components of public sector size, we test two distinct models — one framed as a responsive government interpretation, the other developed to reflect the excessive government perspective. This will give us some basis for evaluating the relative merits of these two different interpretations of growth in the public sector.

Despite the failure of the existing explanations of government growth to account for the actual changes in the size of the public sector, we do not reject completely the logic of these explanations when developing our own models. Indeed, we find that in many cases, the logic underlying an explanation of government growth is much more compelling when it is applied to individual components of government activity than when it is unrealistically asked to account for government in aggregate.

EXPLANATIONS OF PUBLIC SECTOR COST GROWTH

In Chapter 2, the many difficulties involved in developing adequate measures of the size and growth of government were discussed. Among the most important of these was the problem of distinguishing between increases in the scale and scope of government activity and increases in the cost of public sector goods and services relative to those in the economy as a whole. And indeed, when the two sources of the government growth were empirically separated, we saw that the latter, cost growth, accounts for much of the nominal growth of government in the postwar era. Accordingly, any explanation of government growth must include some account of why the costs of publicly provided goods and services have increased at a faster rate than the costs of goods and services provided in the private economy.

Unfortunately, for all its size and breadth, the existing literature says little about this aspect of government growth. That is, nearly all the existing explanations of the government growth process address increases in the real size of government. But there are two exceptions. The bureau voting explanations, presented in Chapter 3, posit that government employees attempt to use their electoral power to win wage gains. As such, the bureau voting explanation implies that the voting power of public employees, by pushing up public sector wages, may be responsible for the dramatic cost growth in the postwar era. This argument constitutes an excessive government interpretation of cost growth.

A second explanation can be viewed as a responsive government interpretation of cost growth. It focuses attention away from the selfish interests of government employees and toward the character of public sector services, in particular, the high degree of labor intensiveness associated with the production of public services. Beck (1976; 1979) suggests that the need to keep wages in the public sector competitive with private sector wages, in concert with the difference in labor intensiveness between the two sectors, is responsible for the bulk of cost growth over the last four decades. In this chapter, we formalize and then test these excessive government and responsive government interpretations of cost growth.

The Responsive Government Model of Cost Growth

This explanation of cost growth is derived from Beck's (1976; 1979) application of Baumol's (1967) study of the growth of city expenditures to the analysis of public sector cost growth. Baumol develops his model by assuming a two sector economy, with one sector that is labor intensive and one that is capital intensive. The capital-intensive sector experiences a regular replacement of capital over time. This replacement facilitates regular productivity improvements in that sector. And these productivity improvements finance both higher profits and higher wages.

In contrast, the labor-intensive sector is expected to possess fewer opportunities for productivity enhancement. Accordingly, there will be no internal pool of resources with which to finance higher wages. But if wages were to increase in the capital-intensive sector, but not in the labor-intensive sector, there would be a flow of labor to the capital-intensive sector; in search of higher wages, labor would move from one sector to the other. The labor-intensive sector would be faced with the possibility of labor shortages and the certainty of attracting only the least competitive members of the labor force. To prevent this scenario, Baumol argues that the labor-intensive market must offer wage increases comparable to those in the capital-intensive sector and finance these wage increases externally through higher prices.

If we assume, as does Beck (1976; 1979), that the public sector conforms to the character of Baumol's labor-intensive sector, and that the private sector has the characteristics of Baumol's capital-intensive sector, then Baumol's simple model can serve as an explanation of cost growth. The private sector, according to Baumol's model, would generate regular productivity increases and, thus, higher wages, over time. The public sector would not experience comparable productivity increases. But faced with mandated tasks (for example, police protection, fire protection, national defense) that it simply cannot abandon, the public sector would have to seek external sources, higher taxes, to fund higher wages in order to remain competitive in the labor market. The result is "Baumol's disease" — ever rising taxes and expenditures with little or no change in the level of public services. Furthermore, the cost of providing government goods and services should rise more rapidly than the cost of production in the private sector. The public sector must grow in terms of revenue extraction in order to maintain a constant level of public service activities.

Baumol's hypothesis has been studied extensively, although a simple interpretation of the results remains elusive. Consistent with the hypothesis, a number of analysts have found that the public sector provides a large number of goods and services that are labor intensive, and therefore, is less likely to generate productivity improvements than the private sector (Bradford, Malt, and Oates 1969; Spann 1977a).[1] Of course, some who recognize the existence of a productivity differential argue that the continuing labor intensiveness of the public sector and its failure to generate productivity improvements are a function more of bureaucratic ineptitude than the inherent character of public sector work (Spann 1977a). Still, the rates of expenditure growth of government programs with presumed higher rates of productivity growth were found to be smaller than those with presumed lower rates of growth (Spann 1977b), a finding that lends support to the argument that the source of Baumol's disease is the nature of public sector work rather than public sector workers per se.

If the Beck/Baumol hypothesis were correct, then the cost of providing public sector goods and services — relative to costs of production in the economy as a whole — should be strongly and positively related to average wage rates in the private sector. Private sector wage increases would lead to wage increases in the public sector, as the government attempts to remain competitive in the labor market. Then, these public sector wage gains — in the absence of significant increases in productivity — would result in increases in the relative cost of production of government goods and services. Thus, the Beck/Baumol explanation of cost growth implies a positive slope coefficient in the bivariate model

$$\text{RELCOST}_t = B_0 + B_1 \text{WAGEPRIV}_{t-1} + E_t \qquad (5.1)$$

where **RELCOST** is the cost of public sector goods and services relative to those in the economy as a whole, and **WAGEPRIV** is the average private sector wage.[2]

But a closer reading of the Beck/Baumol proposition suggests that private sector wages influence the relative costs of public sector goods and services indirectly. First, increasing wage rates in the private sector are expected to lead to higher wages in the public sector. Second, and in turn, public sector wage rates are expected to influence the cost of public sector goods and services relative to those in the overall economy. So a model more correctly specifying the causal process identified in the Beck/Baumol hypothesis contains two equations:

$$\text{WAGEGOV}_t = B_0 + B_1 \text{WAGEPRIV}_{t-1} + E_t{}^1 \text{ and} \qquad (5.2)$$
$$\text{RELCOST}_t = B_2 + B_3 \text{WAGEGOV}_t + E_t{}^2 \qquad (5.3)$$

where **WAGEGOV** is the average public sector wage, and B_1 and B_3 are both positive. Private sector wages are modeled as having a lagged effect on public sector wages to allow time for the labor market to generate sufficient competitive pressures to compel the public sector to augment wages. However, no lag is expected in the impact of government wages on the relative costs of government goods and services, because public sector wages are an intrinsic component of such costs.

The Excessive Government Model of Cost Growth

In the previous chapters, we have seen that, with the exception of the Beck/Baumol interpretation, the government growth literature provides virtually no account of the government cost growth phenomenon. We believe this lack results from most of the extant explanations focusing exclusively on what we have defined as real growth. This lack of attention to cost growth has largely precluded the development of an alternative interpretation of the cost growth process that is consistent with the underlying philosophy of the excessive government interpretation. However, one of the many excessive government explanations of the real growth of government has been reinterpreted recently as an explanation of cost growth. Specifically, Buchanan and Tullock (1977) employ the logic of the bureau voting model developed in Chapter 3 to explain cost growth.

In response to the Beck/Baumol view of the cost growth of government, Buchanan and Tullock (1977) have argued that the real source of the growing cost of public sector goods and services (relative to those in the private sector) lies in the voting power of bureaucrats rather than in Baumol's disease. As the number of government employees increases, their growing power as a voting block would allow them to coerce higher wages from elected officials, which in turn, results in an increase in the relative cost of government goods and services. While Buchanan and Tullock present no formal specification, their argument implies the following model as an alternative to the responsive government specification presented in equation 5.1:

$$RELCOST_t = B_0 + B_1 GOVEM_{t-1} + E_t \qquad (5.4)$$

where GOVEM is the size of the public employee voting block. Because the size of this voting block is presumed to be positively related to the relative cost of public sector goods and services, the coefficient B_1 is expected to be greater than zero.

However, as with the responsive government model of cost growth, this excessive government explanation can best be expressed as a two-equation model:

$$\text{WAGERATIO}_t = B_0 + B_1 \text{GOVEM}_{t-1} + E_t{}^1 \text{ and} \tag{5.5}$$
$$\text{RELCOST}_t = B_2 + B_3 \text{WAGERATIO}_t + E_t{}^2 \tag{5.6}$$

where **WAGERATIO** denotes the ratio of the average public sector wage to the average private sector wages, and B_1 and B_3 are both expected to be positive. First (in equation 5.5), the size of the government employee voting block influences the relative wage rate in the public sector; public sector wages should increase relative to those in the private sector as public employee voting power increases. Then (in equation 5.6), an increase in the average public sector wage relative to that in the private sector results in an increase in the relative cost of public sector goods and services.

TESTING THE MODELS OF COST GROWTH

Introduction

To assess the utility of the responsive and excessive explanations of cost growth, we can estimate coefficients for the model of equations 5.2 and 5.3 and for the model of equations 5.5 and 5.6 separately. If one model clearly works, while the predictions of the other are clearly disconfirmed, we can claim evidence for the superiority of the former. But if the empirical results are not so dramatic, it may be difficult to determine the relative success of the responsive and excessive models because each contains a different intervening variable.

Thus for an additional comparative assessment of the two explanations, we estimate coefficients for an equation, with dependent variable **RELCOST**, that includes as predictors the exogenous variables in the two models: the average private sector wage and the size of the government employee voting block:

$$\text{RELCOST}_t = B_0 + B_1 \text{WAGEPRIV}_{t-1} + B_2 \text{GOVEM}_{t-1} + E_t \tag{5.7}$$

The responsive government interpretation of cost growth leads to an expectation that B_1 is positive and B_2 is near zero, as the responsive view would predict no substantial effect of government employment on the relative cost of public sector goods and services. Conversely, the excessive government interpretation suggests the expectation of a positive value for B_2 but a near zero value for B_1.

Operationalizing the Models

As with our earlier analyses, variables are operationalized with annual data for the period 1948 to 1982. The specific equations to be estimated are the two-equation responsive government (5.2 and 5.3) and excessive government (5.5 and 5.6) models, as well as the single-equation model (5.7) containing the exogenous determinants of both interpretations of cost growth. In operational form, these equations become

The Responsive Government Model

$$\text{wagegov}_t = b_0 + b_1\text{wageman}_{t-1} + e_t \tag{5.7a}$$
$$\text{wagegov}_t = b_2 + b_3\text{wagepriv}_{t-1} + e_t \tag{5.7b}$$
$$\text{relcost}_t = b_4 + b_5\text{wagegov}_t + e_t \tag{5.8}$$

The Excessive Government Model

$$\text{wageratio}_t = b_6 + b_7\text{govem}_{t-1} + e_t \tag{5.9}$$
$$\text{relcost}_t = b_8 + b_9\text{wageratio}_t + e_t \text{ and} \tag{5.10}$$

The Combined Model

$$\text{relcost}_t = b_{10} + b_{11}\text{wagepriv}_{t-1} + b_{12}\text{govem}_{t-1} + e_t \text{ and} \tag{5.11a}$$
$$\text{relcost}_t = b_{13} + b_{14}\text{wageman}_{t-1} + b_{15}\text{govem}_{t-1} + e_t \tag{5.11b}$$

where each of the indicators is defined in Table 5.1.

The ultimate dependent variable in all models is the cost of providing public sector goods and services relative to those in the economy as a whole: RELCOST_t. This is operationalized by the ratio of the implicit price deflator for state, local, and federal government purchases to the implicit price deflator for the gross domestic product for year t. An increase in this ratio of price deflators would indicate that costs in the public sector have risen relative to those in the overall economy. Note that the price deflator in the numerator refers just to government purchases, and not to transfers. Only purchases are considered because the logic of both the responsive and excessive interpretations of cost growth applies solely to purchases. The responsive government view emphasizes the labor intensiveness of public sector work and the resulting limited opportunities for productivity improvement and, thus, focuses on the nature of government purchases. Similarly, the excessive government interpretation rests on the assumption that self-interested government employees use their voting power to extract higher wages. Such wages represent purchases rather than transfers.

The remaining variables in the responsive government model to operationalize are average public and private sector wages, **WAGEGOV** and **WAGEPRIV**. The indicator **wagegov** is the average annual compensation of public sector employees. The choice for the indicator of private sector wages is not as clear cut because there is some controversy over the appropriate wage leader for public sector wages. Baumol (1967) suggests that the manufacturing sector (the most capital-intensive sector) is the wage leader against which public employee wages are compared. However, given the diversity of tasks undertaken by the public sector, it might be more reasonable to view the private sector as a whole as the appropriate referent against which government employee wage scales are pegged. Consequently, in the tests that follow, we employ two measures of private sector wages. **Wageman** is the average annual compensation of employees of manufacturing industries; **wagepriv** is the average annual compensation of employees not working for the government.

In the excessive government model, the size of the public employee voting block is measured as in Chapter 4 with **govem**, the percentage of the voting age population employed by government. The indicator for the ratio of public to private sector wages is **wageratio**, the average annual compensation of government employees divided by the average compensation of private sector employees.

All equations (5.7a through 5.11b) were estimated first using ordinary least squares (OLS) regression. But an analysis of partial autocorrelation coefficients and correlograms indicated a strong likelihood of serial correlation in the form of first-order autoregressive processes. So pseudo-GLS is used to obtain the ultimate coefficient estimates.

Findings

Table 5.2 reports results for both the responsive government model of cost growth (that is, equations 5.7a, 5.7b and 5.8) and the excessive government model (equations 5.9 and 5.10). The evidence in support of the responsive government view is very strong. First, the responsive interpretation suggests that increases in private sector wages prompt similar increases in the public sector. The results in columns 1 and 2 are consistent with this prediction; there are strong positive relationships between the average public sector wage (**wagegov**) and the average wage in both the manufacturing sector (**wageman**) and the private sector as a whole (**wagepriv**). Indeed the R-square coefficients for these relationships both exceed .80.

Second, the responsive government view sees the wage increases in the public sector as responsible for the increase in the cost of that sector's goods and services relative to costs in the economy as a whole. As seen in column 3, a strong positive coefficient is obtained when relative costs of production (**relcost**) is regressed on public sector wages (**wagegov**) — strong enough to yield an R-square of .93. This result is consistent with the second aspect of the responsive government interpretation. Consequently, taken together, the three equations analyzed provide strong support for the responsive government interpretation of cost growth.

As seen in the last two columns of Table 5.2, the support for the two-equation specification of the excessive government interpretation is substantially weaker. There is evidence that an increase in the wages of public sector employees relative to those in the private sector (**wageratio**) is associated with an increase in the relative cost of public sector goods and services (**relcost**) as predicted by the excessive government view; the slope coefficient in column 5 is positive and significant at the .05 level. But the R-square of .18 for the relationship is substantially weaker than we have seen for the equations testing the responsive government model.

Furthermore, there is virtually no support for the other link in the causal chain predicted by the excessive view: the hypothesis that increases in government employee voting power (**govem**) prompt increases in the relative wages of public sector employees (**wageratio**). The results in column 4 show that although the ratio of public sector to private sector wages is positively related to the size of the government employee voting block, the relationship is quite weak, yielding an R-square of only .02. Thus the evidence regarding the excessive government interpretation of cost growth is at best mixed. Moreover, even if some support can be claimed for the excessive view, that support pales when compared to the evidence in favor of the responsive government interpretation.

This assessment of the superiority of the responsive government interpretation of cost growth is reinforced by the results for the equations (5.11a and 5.11b) containing the exogenous determinants from both interpretations as seen in Table 5.3. Using either the average manufacturing wage (column 1) or the average wage in the overall private sector, the cost of government goods and services relative to those in the full economy is positively and strongly related to private wages, consistent with the responsive government interpretation. In contrast, the coefficients for the power of the public employee voting block (**govem**) in both columns 1 and 2 are much weaker, failing a test of significance at the .05 level in both cases, and being very near zero in column 2.

CONCLUSION

For the first component of government growth, growth in the cost of government goods and services relative to costs in the overall economy, the responsive interpretation proves superior to the excessive government view. The results were uniformly supportive of the responsive interpretation derived from the analyses of Baumol and Beck. In contrast, only very weak support was found for the excessive government interpretation. Thus, a very simple model that attributes much of government growth not to the selfish behavior of government employees, but instead to the basic nature of public sector goods and services — in particular, the inherent labor intensiveness of much government activity — works very well. Our results suggest that cost growth results simply from an objective need by government to raise the wages it pays to stay competitive with the private sector labor market.

We must be cautious in the extent to which we can use the strong empirical support for the responsive government interpretation of cost growth, and the weak support for our excessive government model, to reject the broader excessive interpretation of government growth. For example, we cannot reject with certainty the possibility that even though private sector wages may be the principal determinant of government wage levels (as our responsive interpretation suggests), public sector wages are "overindexed" to private wages as they grow together over time. If such overindexing occurs, one can certainly argue that government cost growth is excessive.

Fortunately, some of our empirical results bear on this possibility. The coefficient 1.12 obtained when regressing the average public sector wage (**wagegov**) on the average private sector wage (**wagepriv**) is not substantially greater than 1.00 (see column 2 of Table 5.2). Furthermore, the coefficient .85 (in column 1) for average manufacturing wage (**wageman**) is actually slightly below 1.00. This suggests that public sector wages as an aggregate have increased at just a slightly greater rate than private sector wages and at a slightly lower rate than manufacturing wages. Thus, there is certainly no evidence of the kind of broad-scale overindexing of government wages to private wages in the postwar era that would warrant a conclusion of excessive public sector wage hikes. But our results are at an extremely high level of aggregation. And, certainly, further analysis at a lower level of aggregation, which compares public and private wage scales for more specific types of employment, is needed to offer a more definitive conclusion.

Nevertheless our finding that the responsive interpretation of government cost growth is superior to the excessive interpretation is quite important given the size of this component of government growth. As noted in Chapter 2, much of the nominal growth of government over the postwar period has been in the form of higher costs of government purchases (relative to costs in the private sector) rather than increases in the real scope of government activity.

NOTES

1.   Tullock (1977) and Orzechowski (1974) have challenged the assessment that the public sector is more labor intensive than the private sector. But their evidence is so highly aggregated that it is but a weak challenge to the Baumol model.

2.   In most models developed in Part III, we believe the causal variables included have a delayed, as opposed to immediate, impact on the size of government. Consequently, most independent variables in equations are lagged one year behind the dependent variable.

TABLE 5.1
Description of Indicators Used to Test the Models of Government Cost Growth

Variable	Indicator
govem	Number of full- and part-time (national, state and local) government employees as a percentage of voting-age (i.e., 20 years or older) population
relcost	Ratio of the IPD for government purchases to the IPD for gross domestic product
wagegov	Total real annual compensation of employees of government and government enterprises divided by the number of FTE employees of government and government enterprises (in tens of thousands of dollars)
wageman	Total real annual compensation of manufacturing industries divided by the number of FTE manufacturing employees (in tens of thousands of dollars)
wagepriv	[Total real annual compensation of employees of all industries minus total real compensation of employees of government and government enterprises] divided by [the number of FTE employees of all industries minus the number of FTE employees of government and government enterprises] in tens of thousands of dollars
wageratio	Ratio of wagegov to wagepriv

Notes: IPD is an abbreviation for implicit price deflator; FTE is an abbreviation for full-time equivalent. All IPDs are fixed at 100 in their base year, 1972.

Source: CITIBASE.

TABLE 5.2
Results for the Responsive and Excessive Government Models of Cost Growth

Column:	(1)	(2)	(3)	(4)	(5)
Equation No.:	5.7a	5.7b	5.8	5.9	5.10
			Dependent Variable		
Independent Variable	$wagegov_t$	$wagegov_t$	$relcost_t$	$wageratio_t$	$relcost_t$
$wageman_{t-1}$	$.85^{***}$ (.07)				
$wagepriv_{t-1}$		1.12^{***} (.06)			
$wagegov_t$			$.049^{***}$ (.002)		
$govem_{t-1}$				$.55$ (.69)	
$wageratio_t$					$.74^{*}$ (.28)
Intercept	.31	-.89	.51	.93	.18
R^2	.81	.92	.93	.02	.18
n	(34)	(34)	(35)	(35)	(35)

$^*p < .05$; $^{**}p < .01$; $^{***}p < .001$.

Note: All coefficients are unstandardized; standard errors are in parentheses below coefficients. All equations are estimated using pseudo-GLS and assuming an autoregressive (AR) error structure of order 1.

Source: Compiled by the authors.

TABLE 5.3
Results for the Combined Model Assessing the Responsive and Excessive Interpretations of Cost Growth

Column:	(1)	(2)
Equation No.:	5.11a	5.11b
	Dependent Variable	

Independent Variable	relcost$_t$	relcost$_t$
wageman$_{t-1}$	.045*** (.005)	
wagepriv$_{t-1}$		.058*** (.005)
govem$_{t-1}$	.43 (.59)	.022 (.569)
Intercept	.45	.44
R^2	.87	.91
n	(34)	(34)

*p < .05; **p < .01; ***p < .001.

Note: All coefficients are unstandardized; standard errors are in parentheses below coefficients. All equations are estimated using pseudo-GLS and assuming an autoregressive (AR) error structure of order 1.

Source: Compiled by the authors.

6

GROWTH IN THE SCOPE OF GOVERNMENT PURCHASES

INTRODUCTION

That much of the nominal growth in the public sector in the United States is due to increases in the cost of public sector goods and services relative to those of the economy as a whole in no way lessens the need to develop an explanation of the growth or decline in government's real share of GDP. The freedom and efficiency issues addressed in Chapter 1 remain, even if the magnitude of real government expansion is not as great as originally supposed. In developing such an explanation, we start by drawing the critical distinction between two fundamentally different types of government activity: transfer payments to individuals and direct purchases of goods and services by government.

In making transfer payments, government is collecting money from taxpayers and redistributing it directly to individuals. In making purchases, government buys labor and capital resources and uses them to produce goods and services. Although these two types of activity may, in some instances, be functional substitutes for one another, their differences are probably sufficient to require separate explanations to account for their patterns of change in the postwar period.

First of all, the incentives for government employees concerning transfers may be very different from those concerning purchases. For instance, according to the excessive government view, public sector employees may be motivated by the goal of higher wages and other benefits like more staff to supervise and more office space (Niskanen 1971; Tullock 1977). Because such benefits involve increases in purchases, public employees may face a powerful incentive to try to increase purchases. But government employees are not likely to derive substantial direct personal benefits from increased transfer payments; therefore, they may have considerably less incentive to seek boosts in transfers.

There are also differences in the incentives for elected public officials between transfers and purchases. One concerns the degree to which the two types of expenditures can be manipulated for the electoral benefit of politicians. Specifically, purchases are more "lumpy" than transfers, suggesting that purchases are harder to control in the short term and, therefore, more difficult to manipulate for electoral advantage. A July vote by a member of Congress to increase October Social Security checks should yield more benefit on election day than a vote to increase the appropriation for a communications satellite that may not come on stream for several years.

Moreover, increases in transfer payments adopted for electoral advantage have an effect on the size of the public sector of different scope from that of increases in purchases. Especially when involving changes in entitlement formulas, boosts in transfers are more likely than increases in purchases to have long-term effects on the budget. When a benefit level is increased, the new level becomes the base for future adjustments. In contrast, although the spending involved may be spread over many years, electorally motivated purchases of the type traditionally identified as "pork barrel" eventually end. Once a dam is built, for instance, it does not need to be built again. This difference implies that electorally timed spending increases for the two types of activities may have quite different effects on the long-term growth of government.

Public attitudes about government growth also seem to differ substantially from purchases to transfer payments. Given the negative esteem in which bureaucrats are often held, the public could well be more supportive of government growth in the form of increased transfer spending than in the form of higher levels of labor purchases. Indeed, in their cross-national assessment of welfare backlash, Hibbs and Madsen (1981, p. 434) conclude that, "On the expenditure side, political troubles are caused when state resources are channeled into labor-intensive, government supplied services [that is, purchases] rather than in cash transfers to households."

These differences combine to suggest that transfers and purchases be examined separately. In this chapter, we develop and test two explanations of the scope of government purchases. One is consistent with the underlying assumptions of the responsive interpretation of government growth. In developing this explanation, we focus attention on external sources of demand for growth in public sector purchases. The other explanation is based on the excessive government interpretation. Here, we turn attention away from sources of demand external to government and consider those generated internally. Empirical tests of these two explanations permit us to assess the relative merits of the two fundamental perspectives on the causes of public sector growth. Comparable explanations of the scope of government transfers are developed and tested in the following chapter.

Within the category of government purchases, the scopes of domestic and defense purchases have had strikingly different trends in the post-war period. Figure 2.7 shows that the domestic purchases share of GDP has risen throughout most of the period. In contrast, in most years, the real defense purchases share of GDP has been declining (see Figure 2.8). This simple empirical difference makes it unlikely that we would be able to explain the entirety of government purchases with a single (responsive or excessive) model. Thus, for both our responsive explanation and our excessive interpretation, we develop separate models for the scope of domestic purchases and the scope of defense purchases. The basic structures of the defense and domestic models will be similar. For example, for the responsive explanation, both the domestic and defense models will reflect an analysis of the sources of external demand for purchases growth. And both the excessive domestic and excessive defense models will emphasize internal sources of demand for growth. However, we will see that the specific sources of demand relevant in the domestic arena are different from those in the defense sector.

EXPLAINING THE SCOPE OF GOVERNMENT DOMESTIC PURCHASES

A Responsive Government Interpretation of Domestic Purchases

In formulating a responsive model of domestic purchases, we must analyze the external sources of demand for growth in government purchases. Undoubtedly, Wagner's Law (Wagner 1877) is the most often cited explanation of public sector growth that emphasizes demand factors. The law identifies several factors accompanying industrialization as the key reasons for public sector expansion.

Wagner's Law, which was developed in the nineteenth century, might not help in understanding the causes of government growth in the post–World War II period. Wagner's analysis expressly applied to nations undergoing industrialization, and not to countries like the postwar United States that are in a postindustrial mode of economic development. Indeed, Abizadeh and Gray's (1985) comparison of empirical assessments of the law supports this view; the law appears to hold for developing, but not developed or undeveloped nations. Thus, we need to reexamine the logic underlying Wagner's Law to assess the degree to which it is still applicable in the postindustrial setting of the United States. Chapter 3 discussed three distinct elements of Wagner's Law. We examine each in turn.

One component of Wagner's Law suggests that the income elasticity of public sector spending is greater than one (Mann 1980, p. 189; Borcherding 1977b; Bird 1971). That is, the demand for public sector spending is expected to increase as personal incomes rise, and at a rate faster than income. Of the law's three elements, this one probably has the most relevance to understanding domestic purchases growth in a postindustrial setting. It is possible that many of the amenities of life provided by government in an advanced industrial society are affordable only after the population achieves the affluence associated with postindustrialization (Thurow 1980). Among these amenities may be parks and other recreational facilities, libraries that move beyond the book-lending function to serve as community cultural centers, and a clean environment. All of these amenities involve public sector purchases. Consequently, our responsive government model hypothesizes that the scope of domestic purchases is positively related to societal personal income in the postwar era.

Second, Wagner's Law suggests that the process of industrialization accelerates the need for public goods production as a result of the urbanization and increased interdependencies of modernizing society (Borcherding 1977b). Unlike the income elasticity effect, we expect that the logic of this aspect of Wagner's Law better accounts for purchasing patterns of newly industrializing societies than it does for postindustrial government growth. Quite simply, the concentration of population associated with industrialization and the resulting social interdependencies that are hypothesized to be sources of demand were largely accomplished by the beginning of the postwar era in the United

States. Thus, if this element of Wagner's Law is to be helpful in understanding postwar changes in the scope of domestic purchases, it must be reinterpreted for the postindustrial setting.

And we believe that such a reinterpretation is appropriate. At the heart of the interdependencies component of Wagner's Law is the assertion that changes in social demographics create new demands for public goods and services production. In Wagner's time, the demographic changes associated with industrialization may have been critical. However, even if the United States is no longer experiencing episodes of fundamental demographic change driven by industrialization, it is undoubtedly experiencing other kinds of demographic shifts that may have dramatic effects on the level of demand for government goods and services. The most important of these demographic changes concerns income distribution, household composition, and the age structure of the population.

Not all these changes lead to greater demands for government purchases. Certainly, the "graying" of the U.S. population has led to demands for increased government activity. But for the most part, these demands appear to have been answered with greater transfer spending (for example, Social Security and Medicare). Similarly, if the U.S. government has responded to demands to address problems in income distribution, this response, too, has been in the form of increased transfer activity, through programs such as Aid to Families with Dependent Children (AFDC), and Supplemental Security Income Assistance (SSI). For this reason, demographic variables measuring the size of the elderly and poor populations will be included in the responsive government transfers model presented in Chapter 7.

Other demographic changes, however, are more likely to be associated with demand for government purchases. Two are directly relevant to our effort to explain the scope of domestic purchases.[1] The most important is the size of the population younger than working age. "Baby booms" and "baby busts" should lead to dramatic fluctuations in the level of demand for public sector purchases for such activities as education and police protection (Muller 1984; Peters 1980; Rose 1980). Indeed, new schools were built in the United States after the baby boom, and they were followed shortly by new prisons in response to the increase in crime associated with the baby boom cohort entering young adulthood. But by the 1980s, both the need for more classrooms and the crime rate began to fall.

Household composition has shifted dramatically since World War II. Specifically, the number of households has increased substantially. Muller (1984, p. 133) believes this increase is due to several factors, including "the number of young adults added to the population, marriage and divorce rates, changes in life style, and the financial ability of potential households to own or rent housing." Although total population is sometimes included in empirical tests of Wagner's Law, (see for example, Abizadeh and Gray 1985), the level of public demand for many kinds of domestic purchases (for example, those required for police protection, fire protection, and sanitation) should be more a function of the number of households than the size of the population.

Thus, like Wagner, our responsive government model hypothesizes that demographic factors are important in understanding changes in the level of demand for domestic goods and services. However, our model does not suggest that the process of industrialization is driving the demographic changes leading to increased demand for these goods and services in the postwar United States. Furthermore, our responsive models of public sector growth assume that different demographic factors are associated with changes in the scope of transfers than with changes in the scope of domestic purchases.

The third element of Wagner's Law concerns the technological and infrastructure needs of the industrial economy. The law suggests that an industrial nation requires more capital investment than can be provided by the private sector and, therefore, that government must take a major role in financing capital development. Of course, the demand for the transportation and communication infrastructure that Wagner hypothesized is clearly less relevant for understanding the postwar U.S. experience than for analyzing public sector expansion in newly developing states. But if the object of demand changes, the relationship between the private sector's demand for public sector capital investment and infrastructure support should continue even in a postindustrial setting.

Specifically, the changing mix of economic activity associated with the prospects and problems of advanced industrialization has created a whole new series of investment needs that government is called upon to address. For example, given the heavy demand for skilled labor in an economy dominated by high-tech and service industries, the labor replacement function of public education becomes a critical economic investment. The growing role of government in research and development and the amelioration of costs associated with deindustrialization result from the same pressures. In short, Wagner's insight on the relationship of industrialization and the infrastructure support function of domestic public purchases may be valid even if the United States has passed beyond the early and mid-stages of industrialization to become an advanced industrial economy.

However, the type of response to these infrastructure needs apparently adopted in the United States suggests that they are not relevant for explaining the scope of domestic purchases. Quite simply, a postindustrial government has at least two basic strategies it can employ in addressing this new form of demand for infrastructure support. It can, like several European nations, provide the new forms of infrastructure support directly, through public sector purchases (Lieber 1982). Alternatively, a government can use its tax system to create incentives for private sector solutions of the problem, through so-called "tax expenditures." And although the U.S. response to these demands may have aspects of both strategies, primary reliance has been placed on the latter (McIntyre and Tipps 1983; Plaut and Pluta 1983). But such tax expenditures are not included in the measures of the size of the public sector used in this chapter. Accordingly, we will not incorporate a measure of infrastructure needs in our responsive model of the scope of domestic purchases.

Our model also views the scope of domestic purchases as responsive to public opinion as reflected in electoral outcomes. As Downs (1960) and others have argued, the size of the public sector is determined by citizens' demand for government spending, which is revealed in their choices for parties in elections. Specifically, the responsive government model hypothesizes that control of government by a liberal party results in more extensive public sector purchasing activity than does conservative party control because liberal parties can be expected to favor a stronger government role in domestic economic activity.

Admittedly, this role may be expressed in some forms of activity that involve relatively little expenditure; the regulation of private economic interactions is perhaps the most prominent example. But even regulatory activity involves some level of increased public purchases, as illustrated by the establishment of agencies such as the Environmental Protection Agency, the Office of Surface Mining, and the Office of Price Stability. Moreover, many forms of government involvement in economic and social interactions require more direct action, such as those associated with the line functions of the Energy, Labor, and Education Departments.

The empirical analysis of Chapter 4 offers little support for the hypothesis that party control is a determinant of total government expenditures as a percentage of GDP. But we are not prepared to exclude the party control hypothesis from our responsive government model on this basis. Indeed, we believe the lack of support for the hypothesis may be due to party control having a different type of effect on different components of the size of government — for instance, domestic purchases and defense purchases. Although the responsive interpretation of government growth proposes that liberal party control generates broader domestic purchasing activity than conservative party control, it suggests that liberal control should be associated with a smaller defense purchases share of GDP. If this were the case, the impact of party control might be masked when its relationship to the ratio of total expenditures to GDP is assessed.

Considerable literature also supports a claim of a different type of electoral effect on the size of government, one in which patterns of government expenditures are influenced by the timing of elections, as politicians seek electoral advantage from their spending decisions (see the discussion of the electoral competition explanation in Chapter 3). But in contrast to the transfers models we develop in Chapter 7, we do not include this kind of electoral effect in our responsive government purchases models (either the domestic or defense versions). This may seem somewhat surprising given the popular conception of rampant pork barrel spending for both defense and domestic purchases.

The exclusion of an electoral effect is based on several independent considerations. First, Arnold (1978, cited in Larkey, Stolp, and Winer 1984, p. 78) argues that such projects make up only a small proportion of total government expenditures. Second, pork barrel politics seems to have more influence on the placement of domestic and military installations than on the overall level of purchases (Arnold 1979; Rundquist 1980). Thus, even if pork barrel programs are important politically, they are not relevant for our analysis of the scope (as opposed to pattern of distribution) of government purchases.

Third, unlike transfer payments, spending for concrete projects is difficult to time for electoral purposes; new water projects and other forms of "pork" require years of lead time. Even if appropriations for such projects are electorally timed (Kiewiet and McCubbins 1985), the actual spending probably extends over several years, both election and nonelection. Therefore, pork barrel appropriations decisions, even if timed for electoral considerations, are unlikely to generate a purchases share of GDP that is related to electoral cycles.

Finally, many pork barrel spending projects tend to occur only once. Once a dam is built, it need not be built again. This stands in sharp contrast to election-timed increases in transfer spending that tend to remain in the budget in the form of increased entitlements after the election is over. Consequently, it may be more reasonable to view the funds used for pork barrel projects as constituting a fairly permanent pool of federal spending that is used to finance new projects over time, rather than as generated from a set of sequential decisions, each of which steadily increases the size of the purchases share.

In any event, we can formalize our responsive government domestic purchases model with the equation

$$\text{DOMESTIC}_t = B_0 + B_1\text{PARTY}_{t-1} + B_2\text{YOUNG}_{t-1} + B_3\text{INCOME}_{t-1} \\ + B_4\text{HOUSEHD}_{t-1} + E_t \qquad (6.1)$$

The dependent variable DOMESTIC_t is the scope of domestic purchases in year t. The independent variables in the model are **PARTY, YOUNG, INCOME, HOUSEHD** and an error term E. **PARTY** is the degree of liberal party control of government. **YOUNG** represents the percentage of the population under working age. **INCOME** is total personal income. Finally, **HOUSEHD** denotes the total number of U.S. households. The responsive government interpretation would predict that all partial slope coefficients in equation 6.1 are greater than zero.

An Excessive Government Interpretation of Domestic Purchases

In developing an excessive government model of the scope of domestic purchases, we no longer focus on sources of demand for growth external to government, but instead emphasize internally generated demands. At the core of the excessive interpretation is the conception that growth in government purchases results principally from self-interested political behavior by government officials. In particular, our model posits that growth in domestic purchases is due to the increased voting power of public employees, their manipulation of citizens' demands for public sector activity through fiscal illusions and government structures that make the public sector highly responsive to these artificial demands.

First, the excessive government perspective leads to an expectation that the size of the public employee voting block should be a determinant of the scope of domestic purchases. Courant, Gramlich, and Rubinfeld (1979) argue that as the share of the electorate employed by government grows, public employees have greater influence over the results of elections. Public employees have a direct interest in the growth of their organizations and programs because such growth creates new opportunities for promotion and advancement and for the perquisites often available in an expanding organization. Consequently public employees are hypothesized to vote in a block for the candidate most likely to support government growth. In this sense, to a large degree, the scope of government purchasing activity is unrelated to demands by the public and instead is a function of public employee demand for purchases.

The excessive government interpretation recognizes that at least some of the growth of government is probably determined exogenously; the public is responsible for at least some portion of the demand for domestic government purchases. But, the excessive interpretation views the public's level of demand as artificial, having been manipulated by politicians for their own selfish interests.

Specifically, our excessive government model hypothesizes that the public's demand for domestic purchases is manipulated in two ways. First, as discussed in Chapter 3, politicians are hypothesized to attempt to escape the dilemma of providing desired services paid for by undesired taxes by adopting fiscally illusionary revenue mechanisms that hide the true burden of taxes (Pommerehne and Schneider 1978; Goetz 1977). This would lead voters to underestimate the costs of government goods and services and, consequently, demand more than would be optimal. This suggests the hypothesis that the more successful public officials are in achieving a fiscal illusion, the greater should be the scope of domestic purchases.

Chapter 4 identifies the major hypothesized sources of fiscal illusion. First, a revenue system heavily reliant on withholding taxes from wages — as compared with one more dependent on direct payment by taxpayers — is argued to lead citizens to underestimate their tax burdens (Enrick 1964, Wagstaff 1965). Next, deficit financing is assumed to lead the public to underestimate the true long-term costs of current government expenditures and, therefore, demand more public goods and services than would be optimal (Buchanan and Wagner 1977; Vickrey 1961). Finally, Craig and Heins (1980) contend that a highly complex tax system (that is, one reliant on a large number of small separate taxes rather than a few larger sources) leads citizens to underestimate their total tax burden and, consequently, demand too much government service.

Second, the level of institutional centralization is expected to influence the level of demand for domestic purchases. Also as discussed in Chapter 3, decentralized fiscal systems have been hypothesized to be less effective in resisting citizen demands for public spending than centralized systems (Grodzins 1960; Cameron 1978). The development of more decentralized systems, through intergovernmental aid or other means, then, should be associated with an increased scope of government purchasing activities. Furthermore, in a decentralized system with multiple levels of government and a high reliance on intergovernmental grants-in-aid, the inherent exchange relationship between spending and taxing no longer exists; a government receiving substantial amounts of intergovernmental aid is likely to spend more than a government forced to raise its own funds through direct taxation of its citizens (Goetz 1977; Heidenheimer 1975, p. 28). Thus, the excessive government interpretation suggests that politicians might be able to manipulate the public's demand for goods and services by adopting tax collection mechanisms that minimize the apparent costs of taxation and by developing institutional structures to render the government more responsive to those demands.

Both aspects of the degree of centralization used in the test of the institutional centralization explanation in Chapter 4 are included in our model. **REVCEN** is the extent to which the U.S. tax collection function is controlled by the national (as opposed to state and local) government. **AID** represents the degree to which government spending is financed by grants-in-aid (as opposed to own-sources of revenue). Given these variables, and the fiscal illusion and public employee voting power hypotheses developed above, we can formalize the excessive government interpretation of domestic purchases growth as follows:

$$\text{DOMESTIC}_t = B_0 + B_1\text{CIVGOVEM}_{t-1} + B_2\text{DEBT}_{t-1} + B_3\text{WHELD}_{t-1}$$
$$+ B_4\text{COMPLEX}_{t-1} + B_5\text{REVCEN}_{t-1} + B_6\text{AID}_{t-1}$$
$$+ E_t \tag{6.2}$$

where **CIVGOVEM** is the share of the electorate employed by government. The fiscal illusion variables are **WHELD**, the proportion of U.S. tax receipts collected through withholding from pay checks;

DEBT, the ratio of government debt to expenditures; and **COMPLEX**, the degree of tax system complexity. The excessive government interpretation predicts that all partial slope coefficients except that for **REVCEN** should be positive; B_5 should be negative.

Government Employment and the Scope of Domestic Purchases

The excessive government interpretation postulates that the size of the public employee voting block is a determinant of the scope of domestic purchases. Clearly, the size of the government employee population is empirically related to the scope of domestic purchases. This is because, ceteris paribus, the addition of employees to the civilian public sector work force results in an increase in spending for domestic labor purchases, which, in turn, represent a substantial component of total domestic purchases. However, determining the chain of causation that is responsible for the positive relationship between the employment level and the scope of purchases is a more difficult matter.

In fact, the responsive government interpretation proposes a causal relationship between the size of the civilian work force and the scope of domestic purchases, a relationship radically different from that hypothesized by the excessive government interpretation. If, as the responsive view suggests, government purchases increase in response to external demands on the public sector — and not because government employees expand purchasing activity to advance their selfish goals — then the size of the government work force should not influence the level of purchases. Instead, the external demands should influence decisions about the appropriate scope of government services. Then, these decisions should guide the choice about the number of persons necessary to provide the services planned. When governments purchase goods and, especially, services, they often are undertaking an activity performed directly by public employees — building a dam, prosecuting criminals, or teaching in the public schools. Thus any demand for increases in government services should create a parallel demand for new employees. This thinking prompts the hypothesis that the scope of domestic purchases is a determinant of the level of civilian government employment, or more formally,

$$CIVGOV^*_t = B_0 + B_1 DOMESTIC_t + E_t \qquad (6.3)$$

where **CIVGOV*** is the share of the U.S. work force employed as civilians by government. The responsive government prediction is that B_1 is positive.

We are aware that this hypothesis seems somewhat trivial and may even be tautological; any increase in the size of the government work force necessarily increases the amount government must pay in labor purchases, thus tending to produce a positive relationship between **CIVGOV*** and **DOMESTIC**. But the danger of tautology can be circumvented by analyzing a revised equation,

$$CIVGOV^*_t = B_0 + B_1 DOMCAPITAL_t + E_t \qquad (6.4)$$

in which the independent variable **DOMCAPITAL** represents the scope of domestic purchases for other than employee compensation. When labor purchases are deleted from total purchases in this way, any remaining positive relationship between government employment and the scope of domestic purchases can no longer be suspected of being tautological because there is no guaranteed relationship between the number of public sector employees and the amount they spend on capital purchases.

Note that the expectation expressed by equations 6.3 and 6.4 is in stark contrast to the excessive government view that the level of public employment is largely unrelated to the external demand for government services. Instead, the employment level is presumed to be determined by the power of government employees, that is, their success in minimizing their work loads and maximizing the size of their voting block. From the excessive government perspective, the public sector work force is padded with little relation to the work at hand. For instance, we should see more teachers to reduce each teacher's time spent in the classroom, even as school enrollments are stable or declining. According to the responsive government interpretation, such padding should not take place.

One implication of this that we can use to test the responsive and excessive government interpretations concerns the relative balance between the capital and labor components of domestic purchases. If increases in the number of public employees are unrelated to citizen demands, as suggested by the excessive government interpretation, we should find increases in domestic purchases biased toward labor (as opposed to capital) purchases; only purchases of labor would serve government employees' interests in lower work loads and expanding the public sector work force to increase their voting power (Buchanan and

Tullock 1977). Therefore, if **DOMCAPITAL** is regressed on the independent variables in equation 6.2 to give

$$DOMCAPITAL_t = B_0 + B_1 CIVGOVEM_{t-1} + B_2 DEBT_{t-1}$$
$$+ B_3 WHELD_{t-1} + B_4 COMPLEX_{t-1}$$
$$+ B_5 REVCEN_{t-1} + B_6 AID_{t-1} + E_t \qquad (6.5)$$

the slope coefficient for **CIVGOVEM** should be near zero in magnitude.

In contrast, if the responsive government interpretation were correct, and additional public employees are hired only when external demands for government services create a need for more workers, increases in labor purchases should be accompanied by increases in capital purchases. For example, if more teachers are hired because of an increase in the student population and, therefore, a greater need for their services, we should find increased labor purchases matched by additional capital purchases for new classroom space. Consequently, if the responsive government interpretation were correct, when we regress domestic purchases excluding government employee compensation on the demand variables in equation 6.1, there still should be positive partial slope coefficient estimates for all variables; increases in demand should prompt increases in capital, as well as labor, purchases. In equation form,

$$DOMCAPITAL_t = B_0 + B_1 PARTY_{t-1} + B_2 YOUNG_{t-1}$$
$$+ B_3 INCOME_{t-1} + B_4 HOUSEHD_{t-1} + E_t \qquad (6.6)$$

where the responsive government prediction is that all partial slope coefficients are positive.

TESTING THE MODELS OF THE SCOPE OF DOMESTIC PURCHASES

Operationalizing the Models

All domestic purchases models are tested using annual data for the period 1948 to 1982. The responsive government interpretation is reflected by equation 6.1 (explaining the scope of domestic purchases), equation 6.6 (accounting for the scope of all domestic purchases except compensation of government employees), and equations 6.3 and 6.4 (which have the size of the government work force as dependent variable). In contrast, the excessive government model is specified with equation 6.2 (predicting the scope of domestic purchases) and equation 6.5 (explaining the scope of domestic purchases for other than employee compensation). When operationalized, these equations take the form:

Responsive Government Equations

$$domestic_t = b_0 + b_1 party_{t-1} + b_2 young_{t-1} + b_3 income_{t-1}$$
$$+ b_4 househd_{t-1} + e_t \tag{6.7}$$
$$domcapital_t = b_0 + b_1 party_{t-1} + b_2 young_{t-1} + b_3 income_{t-1}$$
$$+ b_4 househd_{t-1} + e_t \tag{6.8}$$
$$civgov*_t = b_0 + b_1 domestic_t + e_t \tag{6.9}$$
$$civgov*_t = b_0 + b_1 domcapital_t + e_t \tag{6.10}$$

Excessive Government Equations

$$domestic_t = b_0 + b_1 civgovem_{t-1} + b_2 debt_{t-1} + b_3 wheld_{t-1}$$
$$+ b_4 complex_{t-1} + b_5 revcen_{t-1} + b_6 aid_{t-1} + e_t \text{ and} \tag{6.11}$$
$$domcapital_t = b_0 + b_1 civgovem_{t-1} + b_2 debt_{t-1} + b_3 wheld_{t-1}$$
$$+ b_4 complex_{t-1} + b_5 revcen_{t-1} + b_6 aid_{t-1} + e_t. \tag{6.12}$$

Each of the indicators in these equations is defined in Table 6.1. The scope of domestic purchases is measured by **domestic**, the ratio of government domestic purchases to GDP in real terms. Similarly, **domcapital** is the real ratio of domestic purchases for other than compensation of government employees to GDP. There are four independent variables in equations 6.7 and 6.8. **Party** is the indicator of degree of liberal party control of government developed in Chapter 4 (see equation 4.10) that gives equal weight to the states and the national government. The indicator of personal income, **income**, is also drawn from Chapter 4 (equation 4.7). **Young** is the measure of the proportion of the population under working age; and **househd** is the number of households in the United States.

The number of civilian government employees as a percentage of both the electorate (**CIVGOVEM**) and the work force (**CIVGOV***) is measured by the ratio of the number of nonmilitary public employees to the population over age 20. Finally, the indicators for the remaining independent variables in equations 6.11 and 6.12 are all taken from the earlier tests of the fiscal illusion explanation (equation 4.2) and the institutional centralization explanation (4.6).

We estimate the coefficients for the domestic purchases equations (6.7 through 6.12) using ordinary least squares (OLS) regression when there is no evidence of substantial autocorrelation, and pseudo-generalized least squares (GLS) when the OLS residuals suggest the presence of serial correlation. In all latter cases, the error structure is diagnosed as autoregressive, with the order shown in the table presenting the statistical results.

Findings for the Responsive Government Interpretation

The responsive government interpretation of the scope of domestic purchases predicts that all slope coefficients in equations 6.7 through 6.10 are positive. The results are presented in Table 6.2. The estimation of coefficients is complicated by extreme multicollinearity in equations 6.7 and 6.8: **income** and **househd** are correlated at .98. Therefore, although personal income and number of households are distinct conceptually, in a practical sense, it is virtually impossible to sort out the effects of either on the scope of domestic purchases holding the other constant. To determine how sensitive our results are to this multicollinearity, we supplement the estimates for full equations 6.7 and 6.8 (in columns 1 and 4, respectively) with estimates for equations in which only **income** or **househd** is included; the latter results are presented in columns 2, 3, 5 and 6.

In spite of the multicollinearity, our statistical results offer reasonably strong evidence that the scope of domestic purchases is responsive to demand factors, as the responsive government interpretation predicts. Personal income has the strong positive relationship predicted with both total domestic purchases and domestic purchases for other than employee compensation; indeed, income's coefficient is statistically significant in all equations in which it is included. Similarly, the size of the population under working age is positively related to the scope of domestic purchases. Although the coefficient for **young** fails a test of statistical significance at the .05 level in two of the equations for **domcapital**, its sign is uniformly positive across all equations and statistically significant for all of the equations with **domestic** as the dependent variable. Of course, the high degree of labor intensiveness of classroom education suggests that the size of the young population might be expected to exercise its primary influence on purchases of labor rather than capital. If this were the case, the stronger effect of **young** in equation 6.7 than in equation 6.8 would not be surprising.

The results for number of households are somewhat more ambiguous. In the full versions of both equations 6.7 and 6.8, the parameter estimate for **househd** is less than zero, contrary to the prediction of the responsive government model. But these negative coefficients seem to be a result of the extreme multicollinearity present; when personal income is removed from the equations, the estimates for number of households become strongly positive, with t-ratios in excess of 8. Thus, on balance, the results appear to support the hypothesis that the rise in demand accompanying an increase in the number of households leads to an increase in the scope of government purchasing activity.

In contrast, there is no consistent evidence that party control has the predicted influence on domestic purchases. The coefficient for **party** in equation 6.7 is near zero in the full version and weakly negative when variables are deleted to diminish multicollinearity. Although the coefficient for party control is positive, as predicted, in full equation 6.8, it diminishes to near zero in columns 5 and 6. Hence, the claim that conservative and liberal governments differ in the scope of their domestic purchases activity has no support.

The results for the government employment equations (6.9 and 6.10) of the responsive purchases model are presented in columns 7 and 8. The coefficient measuring the effect of the scope of purchases on civilian government employment in equation 6.9 is very strongly positive as predicted. This relationship may be tautological because government employee wages are a major component of **domestic**. However, when expenditures for compensation of employees are completely removed from the independent variable (to yield **domcapital**), its coefficient remains strongly positive (see column 8). This finding is less likely tautological and suggests that government employment grows along with nonwage purchases. Consequently, the evidence is consistent with the responsive interpretation that government employment grows in response to personnel needs created when choices are made to increase the scope of domestic purchases.

Findings for the Excessive Government Interpretation

The excessive government interpretation of domestic purchases predicts that all slope coefficients, except for revenue centralization in equation 6.11, should be positive; the parameter for **revcen** is expected to be negative. But the excessive interpretation predicts that the slope coefficient for civilian government employment (**civgovem**) should decline to near zero in equation 6.12, the dependent variable of which excludes compensation of public sector employees. The statistical findings for equation 6.11 are contained in Table 6.3 with results for the full model in column 1. Data for **wheld** and **complex** are not available for the period 1948 to 1958. Therefore, the full model is estimated using the shorter time series from 1959 to 1982.

As with the responsive model, there was substantial multicollinearity when estimating coefficients for equations 6.11 and 6.12. Regressing each independent variable in these equations except **debt** on the remaining independent variables yields an R-square value greater than .90. Most of the multicollinearity is due to strong empirical relationships between the two institutional centralization variables, **revcen** and **aid** (correlated at -.90) and two of the three fiscal illusion variables, **wheld** and **complex** (correlated at .93). Consequently, to test the sensitivity of our substantive conclusions to multicollinearity, we estimate four separate versions of equations 6.11 and 6.12 each containing only one of **revcen** and **aid**, and only one of **wheld** and **complex** (see columns 2 through 5). Finally, columns 6 and 7 contain the parameter estimates obtained when both **wheld** and **complex** (and one of **revcen** and **aid**) are excluded from equation 6.11. Their elimination allows for estimation using the full post-1948 time series.

In general, the excessive domestic purchases model fares much more poorly than the responsive model. There is no evidence that any of the fiscal illusion mechanisms promote expansion of domestic public sector purchases. The coefficient for government debt is weak or moderate in most of the seven equations and is uniformly negative, in direct opposition to the prediction of the excessive interpretation. Although the tax withholding variable **wheld** has the hypothesized positive coefficient in the full model, its coefficient becomes negative when **complex** is deleted to overcome multicollinearity (see columns 2 and 3). Finally, the coefficient for tax system complexity (**complex**) ranges from weakly negative to near zero in magnitude across the multiple tests.

The data analysis yields inconsistent results concerning the institutional centralization hypothesis. Contrary to expectations, the coefficient for **aid** is negative in the full equation and near zero in all other versions. But **revcen** has the predicted negative coefficient in all regressions in which it is included, and its effect is statistically significant in two of the equations. Thus, it appears that the more centralized the government's revenue collection structure, the smaller the scope of domestic purchases. But given the lack of support for the hypothesis about reliance on intergovernmental aid, the support for the institutional centralization aspect of the excessive government interpretation must be described as weak at best.

The strongest support for the excessive government interpretation comes in the results for the government employment variable. In all equations, the coefficient for the size of the public employee work force is positive, as hypothesized, and significant at better than the .05 level. This result is consistent with the assertion that growth in government is due to self-interested behavior by public employees. But the excessive view also predicts that when the cost of employee compensation is removed from the measure of domestic purchases to yield **domcapital**, the positive relationship between **civgovem** and the scope of purchases should disappear because government workers should have much less selfish interest in expanding the capital component of purchases. This does not turn out to be the case. Although the full model, with strong multicollinearity, yields a weak negative parameter for **civgovem**, the remaining six versions of equation 6.12 generate strong positive coefficients.[2]

Conclusion

There is much greater support for the responsive government interpretation of domestic purchases growth than for the excessive interpretation. All of the hypotheses for the responsive government model are confirmed except for the party control proposition. Each of the remaining demand factors — personal income, the size of the young population, and the number of households — appears to have the expected effect on the scope of purchases. Furthermore, both the size of the purchases share of GDP and the nonemployee compensation component of it have the anticipated relationship with government employment levels.

We must be cautious when interpreting the coefficients that reflect the relationship between the size of the public sector work force and the scope of domestic purchases. There is a positive coefficient both when **domestic**$_t$ is regressed on **civgovem**$_{t-1}$ in the excessive model and when **civgov***$_t$ is regressed on **domestic**$_t$ in the responsive model; the rationales for expecting a positive relationship in the two models are quite different. Clearly, with the data available, it is difficult to determine which causal conception is valid. But, based on the evidence we have, there is more support for the responsive government interpretation. Our findings are consistent with the view that demand factors directly determine the scope of public sector purchasing activity and indirectly affect the size of the government work force as well through their influence on the decision about the scope of purchases.

EXPLAINING THE SCOPE OF GOVERNMENT DEFENSE PURCHASES

The defense purchases component of the size of government is the element that is most slighted in the existing literature on public sector growth. Most theories of government growth — and most tests of these theories using total expenditures as a percentage of GDP as the dependent variable — rarely analyze the factors that influence the scope of defense purchases. Instead, these theories are developed based on an analysis of the nature of domestic spending. When such theories are then applied to explain the overall scope of government (in both the defense and domestic arenas), the implicit assumption is that the scope of defense purchases is determined in exactly the same manner as the scope of domestic purchases.[3] Our responsive and excessive models of government purchases accept this assumption only to the extent that they presume that the basic natures of the forces determining the scopes of domestic and defense purchases are similar. But the specific natures of these forces are hypothesized to be quite different for defense purchases and for domestic purchases.

A Responsive Government Interpretation
of Defense Purchases

Just as with the responsive government interpretation of domestic purchases, developing a responsive explanation of defense purchases requires us to analyze external sources of demand for growth. Our reinterpretation of Wagner's Law led us to hypothesize that societal personal income and two demographic variables are determinants of the scope of domestic purchases. But neither the general logic underlying our reformulation of Wagner's Law nor these specific variables are relevant to an explanation of the scope of defense purchases. First, personal income is postulated to be positively related with the size of government because there seem to be amenities that governments in advanced industrial nations provide only when the population achieves a high level of affluence and can afford those amenities. These amenities involve domestic purchases, not defense purchases. Similarly, there is no reason to expect that either the population under working age or the number of households should have an impact on the scope of defense purchases. These variables should be associated with demand only for domestic services like education and urban police and fire protection.

What, then, are the likely sources of external demand for growth in defense purchases? Political science has a long tradition of "arms race models," in which the military spending levels of a nation are modeled as a function of the spending levels of its adversaries (Caspary 1967; Richardson 1960; Ostrom 1978). Despite the fact that arms race models have not performed well in empirical tests (Ostrom and Marra 1986), the logic underlying the models remains plausible. Drawing on similar logic, our responsive government interpretation includes the proposition that the level of Soviet defense expenditures in a given year is one determinant of the scope of U.S. defense purchases in the following year.[4]

Our responsive model also predicts that the scope of defense purchases should be greater during periods of conflict than in periods of peace because during conflicts, more military personnel are needed, stockpiles of military weapons are expended, and, in general, higher levels of readiness are required. Such a prediction can be justified using the same logic Peacock and Wiseman (1961) employ in their concentration-displacement explanation, which suggests that military crises can lead to public sector growth (see Chapter 3). But our specification is somewhat different from that of Peacock and Wiseman. Specifically, we do not suggest that the size of government remains at its higher crisis level after the crisis (that is, military conflict) is over. Additionally, we apply the crisis effect solely to the defense purchases share, not to the size of government as a whole. Still, the effect of such important specific events as military conflicts on the defense share is something that our responsive model shares with the concentration-displacement interpretation.

Our model also sees the scope of defense purchases as responding to the attitudes of the electorate to the extent that these attitudes are revealed in election outcomes. And as in the case of domestic purchases, our responsive interpretation predicts that party control of government is a determinant of the scope of defense purchases. But the specific nature of the effect of party control on the scope of defense purchases should be quite different. First, whereas the scope of domestic purchases should be affected by party control at all levels of government (national, state, and local), only party control of the national government should influence the scope of defense purchases, as defense decision making is focused principally at the national level. Second, although liberal party control is hypothesized to produce greater domestic purchasing activity than does conservative party control, we expect the very opposite in the defense sector. Public support for a growing defense posture should be expressed by support for a conservative, rather than a liberal, party. Thus, our responsive government model predicts that the degree of liberal party control of the national government should be inversely related to the scope of defense purchases.

External demands for a build-up of the military can also come from interest groups. Indeed, veterans groups have become increasingly mobilized for political action in the post–World War II period. A responsive government interpretation of the scope of defense purchases should predict that an increase in the size of groups pushing for stronger defense should increase the influence of these groups on public officials. Thus, our model hypothesizes that the size of constituency groups supporting defense spending should be positively related to the scope of defense purchases.[5]

But the responsive government interpretation suggests that not all governments should be equally responsive to promilitary constituency groups. Because conservative parties are ideologically more sympathetic to maintaining a large defense sector than are liberal parties, the effect of these groups should be more pronounced during periods of conservative party control of government and more muted when a liberal party is in power. This logic supports the hypothesis that party control and the size of constituency groups supportive of a military build-up should interact in influencing the scope of defense purchases. In particular, the greater the degree of conservative party control of the national government, the stronger the effect of the size of promilitary groups on the scope of defense purchases.

The above analysis suggests the following formalized responsive government interpretation of the scope of defense purchases:

$$\overset{\frown}{DEFENSE}_t = B_0 + B_1 SOVIET_{t-1} + B_2 CONFLICT_t$$
$$+ B_3 PROMILITARY_{t-1} + B_4 PARTYNAT_{t-1}$$
$$+ B_5[(PARTYNAT_{t-1})(PROMILITARY_{t-1})] + E_t \qquad (6.13)$$

where the dependent variable **DEFENSE** is the scope of defense purchases. The first independent variable is **SOVIET**, which denotes the real level of Soviet expenditures. **CONFLICT** is the intensity of military conflict involving the United States. **PROMILITARY** represents the size of constituency groups supporting a military build-up. Finally, **PARTYNAT** is the degree of liberal party control of the national government, with 0 indicating complete conservative party control and 1 meaning complete liberal control. The coefficients for **SOVIET**, **CONFLICT** and **PROMILITARY** are assumed to be positive; those for **PARTYNAT** and the [(**PARTYNAT**) (**PROMILITARY**)] multiplicative term are presumed negative, with the additional restriction that $-B_5$ is less than B_3; that is, the absolute value of B_5 is less than B_3. This restriction is necessary if the model is to reflect the proposition that the effect of the size of promilitary constituency groups on the scope of defense purchases is positive regardless of party control, but more strongly positive as the degree of conservative control of government increases.

An Excessive Government Interpretation of Defense Purchases

Like its analysis of the scope of domestic purchases, the excessive government interpretation views the scope of defense purchases as determined primarily by internally generated demands. But the specific sources of internal demand are different in the defense sector. The excessive government view sees the voting power of public employees as a key cause of domestic purchases growth. On the surface, the large size of the military population (both enlisted and officer personnel) seems to allow the potential for substantial voting power by military personnel.

But the nature of military employment is quite different from that of civilian government employment. On the civilian side, most civil service government employees view their job as a career and tend to have a high degree of job security. If anyone, it is higher-level employees, senior political appointees, who are most likely to view their government service as temporary. But on the military side, the higher-level employees, the officer corps, tend to see the military as a career. In contrast, enlisted personnel are much more likely to view military service as temporary.[6] For this reason, the interest of lower-level military employees (that is, enlisted persons) in increased defense purchases should be significantly less than their civilian lower-level counterparts' (that is, civil service employees) interest in greater domestic purchases. Career-oriented officers would benefit greatly from rising military spending because increased purchases of both capital (for example, weapons) and labor (enlisted persons) create the opportunity for increased domains of authority and greater chances for promotion.

Given that only the officer corps can be assumed to be committed to the goal of expanding military purchases, any influence of military personnel on the scope of defense purchases cannot reasonably be attributed to the voting power of employees. Enlisted personnel may represent a large pool of potential voters, but not ones that can be expected to form a cohesive block supportive of increased military purchases. Furthermore, the size of the officer corps has never exceeded 420,000 during the postwar period, and the size of this corps as a percentage of the voting age population has always been less than four-tenths of one percent (Department of Defense 1984). Consequently, it would be unrealistic to expect even a perfectly cohesive officer corps at its maximum postwar size to represent a voting block to which political parties have an incentive to respond.

Therefore, if the size of the officer corps has any influence on the scope of domestic purchases, its effect must hinge on something other than voting power. Theorists of group influence have often noted the importance of control over information in affording a group power (Niskanen, 1971). Certainly, military officers possess critical information about weapons systems and military strategy that only they can make available to politicians. This makes military officers potentially quite influential in both the formal and informal lobbying of politicians. For this reason, we hypothesize that the greater the extent to which the military is dominated by its officer corps, the greater the influence of military officers on defense policy. The best indicator of dominance of officers within the military is the number of officers as a percentage of the overall military population. This suggests the excessive government proposition that the greater the percentage of military employees that are officers, the greater the scope of defense purchases.

Our excessive government model of domestic purchases incorporates the fiscal illusion hypothesis. Should an excessive interpretation of the scope of defense purchases do so as well? Because any fiscally illusionary tax collection mechanisms successfully adopted by politicians should produce excess revenues that can be spent on defense as well as domestic programs, the fiscal illusion variables in the excessive domestic purchases model should be included in the defense purchases model as well. However, because defense spending is almost exclusively a federal responsibility, the hypothesis that the degree of institutional centralization affects the scope of public sector purchases — framed in the domestic arena — is not relevant in the defense purchases context.

We therefore specify our excessive government defense purchases model in the following manner:

$$\text{DEFENSE}_t = B_0 + B_1\text{OFFICER}_{t-1} + B_2\text{DEBT}_{t-1} + B_3\text{WHELD}_{t-1} + B_4\text{COMPLEX}_{t-1} + E_t \tag{6.14}$$

where **OFFICER** is the share of the overall military population that are officers, and **DEBT, WHELD**, and **COMPLEX** are defined as in the excessive domestic purchases model; **DEBT** is the ratio of government debt to spending, **WHELD** denotes the percentage of government revenues collected by withholding from pay checks, and **COMPLEX** is the degree of complexity of the tax system. All partial slope coefficients are predicted by the excessive government interpretation to be positive.

Government Employment and the Scope of Defense Purchases

Just as in the domestic sector, the level of employment in the defense sector will be related to the scope of purchases in that sector. Although the defense function in the United States has become increasingly capital intensive because of the greater reliance on nuclear missiles and other "smart weapons," the cost of maintaining the population of the armed forces remains a very large component of the national defense budget. Indeed, personnel costs (including salaries, allowances, moving expenses, and subsidies in kind) totalled $44 billion in 1982 (Arabellera and Labrie 1982). Military personnel costs represent a large component of total defense purchases; therefore, military employment must be correlated with defense purchases over time. The question of concern is what causal relationship, if any, exists between employment and purchases?

The responsive government interpretation would predict a causal relationship between defense purchases and military employment similar in nature to the relationship it foresees between domestic purchases and civilian government employment. Specifically, external demands on government should influence choices about the proper level of national defense, and these choices should, in turn, determine the necessary level of military employment; new people should be hired only when more personnel are needed to provide the level of defense services desired. This logic suggests the responsive government hypothesis that the scope of defense purchases is a determinant of the level of military employment:

$$MILPOP_t = B_0 + B_1 DEFENSE_t + E_t \qquad (6.15)$$

where **MILPOP** is the share of the U.S. work force employed in the military, and the prediction is that B_1 is positive.

Once again, however, we face the danger that any positive coefficient estimate obtained would be tautological because any increase in the military population necessarily results in a boost in the cost of labor purchases. This concern can be overcome with a now familiar strategy — conceptualizing a new variable, **DEFCAPITAL**, the cost of defense purchases for other than employee compensation. Then, if the responsive government interpretation is correct, the regression

$$MILPOP_t = B_0 + B_1 DEFCAPITAL_t + E_t \qquad (6.16)$$

should also yield a positive value for B_1. These military employment equations parallel fully the civilian employment equations, 6.3 and 6.4, developed earlier.

But the process determining the military employment level is more complex than that reflected by equations 6.15 and 6.16 because of a military draft during part of the postwar period. Clearly, a move from compulsory to voluntary recruitment should lead to reduced demand for military personnel. Moreover, during periods of voluntary recruitment, the level of military wages relative to those in the private sector should be an important determinant of the attractiveness of military service and, hence, the level of military employment. In contrast, when military conscription is used, any need for the military to compete with the private sector in the labor market is eliminated. These expectations prompt us to revise equations 6.15 and 6.16 to obtain:

$$\text{MILPOP}_t = B_0 + B_1\text{DEFENSE}_t + B_2\text{DRAFT}_t + B_3\text{RELWAGE}_{t-1}$$
$$+ B_4[(\text{RELWAGE}_{t-1})(\text{DRAFT}_t)] + E_t \qquad (6.17)$$

and

$$\text{MILPOP}_t = B_0 + B_1\text{DEFCAPITAL}_t + B_2\text{DRAFT}_t$$
$$+ B_3\text{RELWAGE}_{t-1} + B_4[(\text{RELWAGE}_{t-1})(\text{DRAFT}_t)]$$
$$+ E_t \qquad (6.18)$$

where **DRAFT** is a dichotomous variable that equals 0 when a draft is operating and 1 otherwise, and **RELWAGE** is the ratio of the average military wage to the average private sector wage. The responsive government prediction is that, in both equations, B_1 and B_4 should be strongly positive; B_3 should be positive, but near zero in magnitude; and B_2 should be negative. A small (but positive) value for B_3 indicates that when a draft exists, the level of military wages relative to those in the private sector should have only a weak positive effect on the level of military employment. But a positive value for B_4, the coefficient for the multiplicative term, implies that the effect of wages on employment should be stronger when there is no draft and all recruitment is voluntary.

We can subject the responsive government interpretation to a further test by examining its expectations regarding the mix of the capital and labor components of defense purchases. The responsive interpretation predicts that additional military employees are recruited only when external demands for defense services result in a need for more personnel. Therefore, any increase in labor purchases should be matched by a comparable rise in capital purchases. This means that the demand variables in equation 6.13 should also have an effect on the capital component of defense purchases. In equation form, this responsive government hypothesis is

$$\text{DEFCAPITAL}_t = B_0 + B_1 \text{SOVIET}_{t-1} + B_2 \text{CONFLICT}_t$$
$$+ B_3 \text{PROMILITARY}_{t-1} + B_4 \text{PARTYNAT}_{t-1}$$
$$+ B_5[(\text{PARTYNAT}_{t-1})(\text{PROMILITARY}_{t-1})]$$
$$+ E_t \tag{6.19}$$

where the partial slope coefficients have signs identical to those in equation 6.13: the coefficients for **SOVIET**, **CONFLICT**, and **PROMILITARY** are positive; those for **PARTYNAT** and [(**PARTYNAT**)] (**PROMILITARY**)] are negative, and the absolute value of B_5 is less than B_3.

The excessive government interpretation of defense purchases does not offer a clear prediction about the relative balance of labor and capital purchases. In the domestic context, the excessive interpretation suggests that the clear preference of government employees is for using additional resources to finance the purchase of labor. This is because additional employees simultaneously increase the size of the public employee voting block and reduce the work load for existing employees. But we have argued that the voting power of military employees should be irrelevant to the process by which the scope of defense purchases is determined.

Instead, we must focus attention on the officer corps, for it is the size and influence of this group that our excessive government interpretation predicts will have an influence on the scope of defense purchases. Certainly, an expansion of the military population through the recruitment of additional enlisted personnel does not reduce the work load of officers. But it does create the need for more officers, and such expansion enhances the probability of promotion within the officer corps. In a parallel fashion, however, expansion of research and development and the procurement of new advanced military hardware also broaden the possibilities for officers' advancement and promotion. So officers seem to have a vested interest in the expansion of purchases of both labor and capital. For this reason, it is impossible to derive an excessive government equation contrasting with responsive equation 6.19 and analogous to the excessive domestic purchases equation 6.5. Our empirical test of the excessive government interpretation of the scope of defense purchases must be limited to analysis based on equation 6.14.

TESTING THE MODELS OF THE SCOPE OF DEFENSE PURCHASES

Operationalizing the Models

As with earlier analyses, all equations are tested with annual data from 1948 to 1982. The responsive government interpretation of defense purchases is specified by four equations, one (6.13) having the scope of defense purchases as dependent variable, one (6.19) having the capital component of the scope of defense purchases as dependent variable, and two (6.17 and 6.18) predicting the size of the military population. In operational form, these equations are

Responsive Government Equations

$$\text{defense}_t = b_0 + b_1 \text{soviet}_{t-1} + b_2 \text{deaths}_t + b_3 \text{vet:vote}_{t-1}$$
$$+ b_4 \text{partynat}_{t-1} + b_5[(\text{partynat}_{t-1})(\text{vet:vote}_{t-1})] + e_t \qquad (6.20)$$

$$\text{milpop}_t = b_0 + b_1 \text{defense}_t + b_2 \text{draft}_t + b_3 \text{relwage}_{t-1}$$
$$+ b_4[(\text{relwage}_{t-1})(\text{draft}_t)] + e_t \qquad (6.21)$$

$$\text{milpop}_t = b_0 + b_1 \text{defcapital}_t + b_2 \text{draft}_t + b_3 \text{relwage}_{t-1}$$
$$+ b_4[(\text{relwage}_{t-1})(\text{draft}_t)] + e_t \qquad (6.22)$$

$$\text{defcapital}_t = b_0 + b_1 \text{soviet}_{t-1} + b_2 \text{deaths}_t + b_3 \text{vet:vote}_{t-1}$$
$$+ b_4 \text{partynat}_{t-1} + b_5[(\text{partynat}_{t-1})(\text{vet:vote}_{t-1})] + e_t \qquad (6.23)$$

Each of the variables in these equations is defined in Table 6.4. **Defense** is the real share of GDP devoted to national defense purchases; **defcapital** is the share of GDP represented by nonlabor purchases of goods and services for defense. The remaining dependent variable, **milpop**, denotes the number of military employees as a percentage of the U.S. work force.

The variable **soviet** is the real level of defense expenditures by the Soviet Union. The quality of available data on Soviet defense expenditures has always been subject to controversy. Also, the data available tend to cover only part of the time period in which we are interested. After examining a number of series, we have chosen to use Ward's (1984, p. 311) estimated USSR defense expenditures as our indicator **soviet**. Ward makes a serious attempt to understand the controversies about this measure in the literature, and his data (for 1951 to 1978) have the added advantage of covering most of the period of interest. Pre-1952 and post-1978 Soviet defense expenditures were interpolated.

The concept of the intensity of military conflict (**CONFLICT**), in equations 6.13 and 6.19, is measured by **deaths**, the number of deaths suffered in military combat; this indicator successfully reflects both the occurrence and severity of military confrontations. Because groups supportive of large military expenditures are typically based on veteran status, the size of constituency groups supporting a military build-up (**PROMILITARY**) is tapped by **vet:vote**, the percentage of the electorate that are veterans of the armed forces. Finally, **partynat** is a measure of liberal party control of the national government ranging from 0 to 1; **draft** is a dichotomous variable equaling 0 when there is a military draft, and 1 when there is not; and **relwage** denotes the ratio of the average military wage to that in the private sector.

When operationalized, equation 6.14 — the excessive government defense purchases model — becomes

Excessive Government Equation

$$\text{defense}_t = b_0 + b_1\text{officer}_{t-1} + b_2\text{debt}_{t-1} + b_3\text{wheld}_{t-1} \\ + b_4\text{complex}_{t-1} + e_t \qquad (6.24)$$

where **officer** represents the number of military officers as a percentage of the total military population, and the remaining independent variables are defined just as in our earlier tests of the fiscal illusion explanation (equation 4.2) and the excessive domestic purchases model.

Findings for the Responsive Government Interpretation

The responsive government interpretation predicts that the coefficients for **deaths**, **soviet**, and **vet:vote** in equations 6.20 and 6.23 are positive, but that those for **partynat** and [(**partynat**) (**vet:vote**)] are negative. As with the equations containing multiplicative terms encountered earlier, attempts to obtain reasonable estimates for the coefficients of equations 6.20 and 6.23 failed because of extreme multicollinearity. Indeed, when either **partynat** or [(**partynat**) (**vet:vote**)] are regressed on the remaining independent variables, the resulting R-square values exceed .99. The least objectionable course for overcoming the multicollinearity in this case seems to be deleting the multiplicative term from the estimation equations, thereby assuming that the partial slope coefficient for the product term is zero. Substantively, this implies the assumption that the effect of the size of promilitary constituency groups on the scope of defense purchases (and its capital component) does not depend on the political party controlling government. The results for these simplified versions of equations 6.20 and 6.23 are presented in Table 6.5, in columns 1 and 2, respectively.

The statistical results offer little evidence that the demand factors in the responsive government model affect the scope of defense purchases in the manner hypothesized. Although the coefficient for the indicator of the intensity of military conflict (**deaths**) is positive as predicted in the equations for both **defense** and **defcapital**, it is very weak in both instances. Furthermore, two other demand factors, Soviet defense expenditures (**soviet**) and the size of promilitary constituency groups (measured by **vet:vote**) actually are negatively related to the scope of defense purchases, with coefficients that are statistically significant in both columns 1 and 2. These coefficients suggest that the scope of defense purchases declines as Soviet defense expenditures increase, and as the size of the veteran population rises. Although these two findings are inconsistent with the responsive government interpretation, the former is certainly consistent with the casual observation that real Soviet defense expenditures have been rising during the last 15 years while the United States was cutting the share of its GDP devoted to national defense.

Of the variables in equations 6.20 and 6.23, only party control seems to have a substantial effect in the direction anticipated on the scope of defense purchases. The negative coefficients for **partynat** in columns 1 and 2 suggest that the scope of defense purchases (and the capital component of defense purchases) tends to be greater when government is controlled by a conservative party than when it is run by a liberal party. This is consistent with the responsive interpretation's proposition that government defense policies should be influenced by the ideological orientations of the dominant party. But note that the coefficients for **partynat** are not statistically significant. If there is an effect of party control on the scope of defense purchases, it is probably not of strong magnitude.

The results for the military employment equations (6.21 and 6.22) of the responsive government model are also presented in Table 6.5. However, once again, we are forced by multicollinearity to report coefficients for restricted versions of these equations. For the full versions, regressing either **draft** or the [(**relwage**) (**draft**)] term on all other independent variables produces an R-square coefficient greater than .99. The best way to proceed when facing such extreme multicollinearity is to employ available theory to assume a value that previously was being estimated. The predictions of the responsive government interpretation are that, for both equations 6.21 and 6.22, the coefficient for **draft** (b_2) should be negative; the coefficients for the scope of defense purchases (b_1) and the product term (b_4) should be positive; and the parameter for **relwage** (b_3) should be positive, but near zero in value. The last of these predictions is consistent with the hypothesis that the relative level of military wages should have very little effect on the level of military employment when a military draft is operating. Thus, for the purposes of estimation, we will treat the coefficient for **relwage** as known, adopting the assumption that it is actually equal to zero. Not knowing precisely what "a small effect" of relative wages on military population means, assuming that effect to be zero seems the most defensible choice.

The results for the military employment equations (Table 6.5) offer substantial support for all hypotheses. First, the coefficient for **draft** is negative in both columns 3 and 4, as anticipated by hypothesis; it is statistically significant at the .05 level in one (column 4) and closely approaches that level in the other. Furthermore, the estimate for the product term, [(**relwage**) (**draft**)], is positive (as predicted) in both columns. Although it is not significant in either column, its t-value exceeds 1.5 in both cases. Taken together, these results for **draft** and [(**relwage**) (**draft**)] imply that the military population is larger when there is a draft than when military service is strictly voluntary and that the influence of military wage levels (relative to those in the private sector) on the size of the military population is weaker when a draft is present than when one is absent.

More substantively relevant for the purposes of evaluating the responsive government interpretation are the findings about the effect of the scope of defense purchases on the size of the military population. As shown in column 3, the coefficient estimate for **defense** is very strongly positive, as predicted. As with the comparable civilian government employment equation (6.9), we should not draw strong conclusions from this finding, given the virtually guaranteed empirical relationship between military employment and the level of defense purchases noted earlier. But column 4 presents results for the analysis in which military wages are excluded from the indicator of the scope of defense purchases, and thus the danger of tautology is lessened. Again, the coefficient for the scope of purchases is quite strongly positive. Consequently, the evidence is consistent with the responsive government view that military employment grows in response to needs created by the policy choice to increase the scope of national defense activity.

Findings for the Excessive Government Interpretation

The excessive government view predicts that all partial slope coefficients in equation 6.24 are positive. GLS produced the following parameter estimates for this equation:[7]

$$\text{defense}_t = .32 - 2.56^{***}\text{officer}_{t-1} - .061\text{debt}_{t-1}$$
$$(.54) \qquad\qquad\qquad (.041)$$

$$- .0055^{***}\text{wheld}_{t-1} + .82^{*}\text{complex}_{t-1}$$
$$(.0012) \qquad\qquad (.33)$$

$$R^2 = .80, n = 23$$

These results offer little support for the fiscal illusion hypothesis. Tax system complexity appears to have the predicted positive impact on the scope of defense purchases; the coefficient for **complex** is positive and statistically significant. But the estimates for the use of tax withholding (**wheld**) and the level of government debt (**debt**) are both contrary to the excessive government prediction, having negative values.

The remaining excessive government hypothesis is that the scope of defense purchases is influenced by the dominance of officers in the military population; in particular, the share of the military population that is officers should be positively related to the scope of defense purchases. However, the empirical evidence is to the contrary. The negative parameter estimate for **officers** suggests that as the size of the officers corps increases (relative to the overall military population), the scope of defense purchases actually decreases. Thus, there is no evidence that greater prevalence of the officer corps in the military results in an expansion of the defense sector.

Conclusion

Frankly, there is little empirical support for either the responsive or the excessive government interpretations of the scope of defense purchases. There are some exceptions to this conclusion. Party control seems to have the effect on the scope of national defense predicted by the responsive government interpretation. But the failure to find empirical evidence that two other demand factors — Soviet defense expenditures and the intensity of military conflict — affect the scope of defense purchases in the manner expected, leaves us unwilling to claim support for the view that the scope of national defense is highly responsive to external sources of demand. The only part of either the responsive or the excessive model to receive substantial support is the responsive government equation specifying the determinants of the size of the military population. There is evidence that the level of military employment is determined by the government's policy concerning a military draft, by the relative level of wages in the military, and by the need for military personnel resulting from policy choices about the appropriate scope of national defense.

NOTES

1. The demographic shifts resulting from postwar population migration also are likely to have a significant influence on public sector domestic purchasing patterns. But these shifts are more important in terms of the spatial distribution of demand for government purchases than in terms of its aggregate size. For example, the postwar suburbanization of the population, migrations from the Sun Belt to the Frost Belt in the 1950s, and the reverse migration of the 1970s seem unlikely to have influenced the domestic purchases share of GDP. Instead, these movements affected the distribution of purchases demand within the country.

2. To save space, we do not present the full set of coefficient estimates for the various versions of equation 6.12. But if the coefficients for equation 6.12 were reported in the exact form of Table 6.3, the row for **civgovem** would be as follows:

Column:	(1)	(2)	(3)	(4)	(5)	(6)	(7)
civgovem	−.13	.46	.57**	.64**	.61**	.53**	.47**
	(.22)	(.23)	(.18)	(.18)	(.17)	(.10)	(.11)

3. The international explanation and concentration-displacement explanations (reviewed in Chapter 3) are two exceptions to the tendency for theories of government growth to focus on domestic sources of growth. Furthermore, while the government growth literature tends to ignore the determinants of the defense purchases share of GDP, the study of defense expenditure levels has a long history (see, for example, Kanter 1972; Ostrom 1978).

4.   We recognize that if, in turn, increases in the scope of U.S. defense purchases prompt increases in Soviet military spending, the exclusion of an equation specifying this reciprocal effect will lead to specification error (and possible bias) when estimating the coefficients of equation 6.13 (Berry 1984). The only solution to this problem would be the development of a nonrecursive model that would include a distinct equation specifying the determinants of Soviet defense expenditures. Because insight on the nature of the Soviet budgetary process is lacking, and because data for the potential determinants of Soviet defense spending would probably not be available, we have no choice but to accept the possible bias that may be present in our coefficient estimates.

5.   Note that we do not introduce a parallel hypothesis about the effect of constituency group size on domestic purchases. This is because the groups with strong interests in domestic policy choices tend to be concerned primarily with policies about government transfers, rather than with choices about purchasing activities. The sizes of several constituency groups (for example, the elderly) will be included as independent variables in our models of government transfers.

6.   This is especially the case during periods in which a military draft is in place.

7.   All coefficients are standardized; standard errors are in parentheses below coefficients. The equation is estimated using pseudo-GLS and assuming a first-order autoregressive error structure.

TABLE 6.1
Description of Indicators Used to Test the Models of the Scope of Domestic Purchases

Variable	Indicator
aid	Federal and state grants-in-aid to state and/or local governments as a percentage of total federal, state and local expenditures
civgovem and civgov*	Number of full- and part-time nonmilitary government employees as a percentage of the over-20 population
complex	Herfindahl Index of Revenue Concentration (see Wagner 1976, p. 55) based on eight revenue sources: corporate profits tax, business nontax revenue, customs revenue, estate gift tax, excise tax, income tax, social insurance contributions, and indirect business tax (data only available for period 1959 to 1982)
debt	[Federal, state and local government expenditures minus federal, state and local receipts] as a percentage of [total federal, state and local government expenditures]
domcapital	Ratio of [(total government purchases of goods and services for other than national defense minus compensation of civilian government employees) divided by IPD for nondefense purchases] to [GDP divided by IPD for GDP][a]
domestic	Ratio of [total government purchases of goods and services for other than national defense divided by IPD for nondefense purchases] to [GDP divided by IPD for GDP][a]
househd	Number of households
income	Total personal income in billions of dollars divided by IPD for national income
party	The average of a state government party control indicator, (G / 2), and a national government party control indicator, ((H / 4) + (S / 4) + (P /2)); where G is the number of nonsouthern Democratic governors divided by the total number of governors; H (or S) equals 1 when the majority party in the United States House (or Senate) is the Democrats, and 0 otherwise; and P equals 1 if the United States president is a Democrat, and 0 otherwise
revcen	[Federal government receipts] as a percentage of [total federal, state and local government receipts excluding grants-in-aid]

149

Table 6.1, Continued

wheld	[Government receipts from social insurance contributions and federal, state and local income taxes] as a percentage of [total federal, state and local government receipts excluding grants-in-aid] (data only available for period 1958 to 1982)
young	Percentage of population less than 18 years old

- -

[a]The IPD for nondefense purchases was not available for the full time period. Accordingly, an estimated IPD for the full period was developed by first regressing the IPD for nondefense purchases on IPDs for total government purchases, federal government purchases, federal government expenditures, and general government expenditures for the period in which all the data were available from CITIBASE (1972 to 1983). Over this truncated time period, the R-square value for the regression exceeded .99. Then the coefficient estimates for the regression equation along with data for the independent variables from 1948 to 1982 were used to generate predicted values for the IPD for nondefense purchases from 1948 to 1982. These predicted values were used in constructing **domestic** and **domcapital**.

Note: IPD is an abbreviation for implicit price deflator; FTE is an abbreviation for full-time equivalent. All IPDs are fixed at 100 in their base year, 1972.

Sources: All data were provided by CITIBASE (maintained by the Economics Department of Citibank) except **househd** and **party**. **Househd** is from *Statistical Abstract of the United States*; **party** is from *Book of the States*.

TABLE 6.2
Results for the Responsive Domestic Purchases Equations

Column:	(1)	(2)	(3)	(4)	(5)	(6)	(7)	(8)
Equation No.:	6.7	6.7	6.7	6.8	6.8	6.8	6.9	6.10
				Dependent Variable				
Independent Variable	$domestic_t$	$domestic_t$	$domestic_t$	$domcapital_t$	$domcapital_t$	$domcapital_t$	$civgov^*_t$	$civgov^*_t$
$party_{t-1}$	-.00047	-.0070	-.0069	.0059	.00042	.00027		
	(.00670)	(.0063)	(.0072)	(.0032)	(.00369)	(.00411)		
$young_{t-1}$	.39***	.34**	.28*	.099***	.079	.059		
	(.07)	(.10)	(.12)	(.026)	(.039)	(.045)		
$income_{t-1}$	.00020***	.00010***		.000087***	.000039***			
	(.00004)	(.00001)		(.000021)	(.000004)			
$househd_{t-1}$	-.0000021*		.0000022***	-.0000011*		.00000086***		
	(.0000010)		(.0000003)	(.0000005)		(.00000010)		
$domestic_t$							.54***	
							(.02)	
$domcapital_t$								1.26***
								(.11)
Intercept	-.03	-.06	-.09	-.00	-.02	-.04	.02	.04
R^2	.93	.82	.73	.93	.82	.76	.97	.81
n	(34)	(34)	(34)	(34)	(34)	(34)	(35)	(35)
Order of AR Process	2	1	1	2	1	1	2	3

*p < .05; **p < .01; ***p < .001.

Note: All coefficients are unstandardized; standard errors are in parentheses below coefficients. All equations are estimated using pseudo-GLS and assuming an autoregressive (AR) error structure with the order indicated in the last row of this table.

Source: Compiled by the authors.

TABLE 6.3
Results for Excessive Domestic Purchases Equation 6.11

Column:	(1)	(2)	(3)	(4)	(5)	(6)	(7)
				Dependent Variable			
Independent Variable	$domestic_t$	$domestic_t$	$domestic_t$	$domestic_t$	$domestic_t$	$domestic_t$	$domestic_t$
$civgovem_{t-1}$	.79* (.35)	1.36*** (.27)	1.71*** (.21)	1.31*** (.21)	1.59*** (.22)	1.36*** (.13)	1.69*** (.23)
$debt_{t-1}$	-.064* (.028)	-.033 (.025)	-.014 (.024)	-.021 (.029)	-.00093 (.02824)	-.022 (.015)	-.010 (.014)
$wheld_{t-1}$	.0022 (.0012)	-.000056 (.000416)	-.00040 (.00041)				
$complex_{t-1}$	-.22 (.19)			.00005 (.07814)	-.053 (.082)		
$revcen_{t-1}$	-.40** (.12)	-.14 (.08)		-.14 (.08)		-.16** (.05)	
aid_{t-1}	-.32 (.15)		.011 (.127)		.012 (.129)		-.0027 (.1507)
Intercept	.31	.10	-.01	.10	.00	.12	-.02
R^2	.97	.96	.96	.96	.95	.98	.93
n	(23)	(24)	(24)	(23)	(23)	(34)	(34)
Order of AR Process	2	OLS	OLS	OLS	OLS	OLS	1

$*p < .05$; $**p < .01$; $***p < .001$.

Note: All coefficients are unstandardized; standard errors are in parentheses below coefficients. Some equations are estimated with ordinary least squares regression; others are estimated using pseudo-GLS and assuming an autoregressive (AR) error structure with the order indicated in the last row of this table.

Source: Compiled by the authors.

TABLE 6.4
Description of Indicators Used to Test the Models of the Scope of Defense Purchases

Variable	Indicator
complex	Herfindahl Index of Revenue Concentration (see Wagner 1976, p. 55) based on eight revenue sources: corporate profits tax, business nontax revenue, customs revenue, estate gift tax, excise tax, income tax, social insurance contributions, and indirect business tax (data only available for period 1959 to 1982)
deaths	Number of combat deaths suffered by United States' armed forces
debt	[Federal, state and local government expenditures minus federal, state and local receipts] as a percentage of [total federal, state and local government expenditures]
defcapital	Ratio of [(national government purchases of goods and services for national defense minus compensation of military employees) divided by IPD for national government defense purchases] to [GDP divided by IPD for GDP][a]
defense	Ratio of [national government purchases of goods and services for national defense divided by IPD for national government defense purchases] to [GDP divided by IPD for GDP][a]
draft	Dichotomous variable which equals 0 when a military draft is operative, and 1 otherwise
milpop	Number of full- and part-time federal government military employees as a percentage of the over-20 population
officers	Number of officers in all military services as a percentage of the number of full- and part-time federal government military employees
partynat	$((H / 4) + (S / 4) + (P / 2))$, where H (or S) equals 1 when the majority party in the United States House (or Senate) is the Democrats, and 0 otherwise; and P equals 1 if the United States president is a Democrat, and 0 otherwise

Table 6.4, Continued

relwage	**wagemil** divided by **wagepriv**, where **wagemil** equals total real annual compensation of military employees of the national government divided by the number of FTE military employees, and **wagepriv** equals [total real compensation of employees of all industries minus total real compensation of employees of government and government enterprises] divided by [the number of FTE employees of all industries minus the number of FTE employees of government and government enterprises]
soviet	Real Soviet Union defense expenditures. For the 1951 to 1978 period, data from Ward (1983: 311) is used; pre-1951 and post-1978 expenditures were interpolated
vet:vote	Number of military veterans as a percentage of the voting-age (i.e., 20 years or older) population
wheld	[Government receipts from social insurance contributions and federal, state and local income taxes] as a percentage of [total federal, state and local government receipts excluding grants-in-aid] (data only available for period 1958 to 1982)

- -

[a]The IPD for defense purchases was not available for the full time period. Accordingly, an estimated IPD for the full period was developed by first regressing the IPD for defense purchases on IPDs for total government purchases, federal government purchases, federal government expenditures, and general government expenditures for the period in which all the data were available from CITIBASE (1972 to 1983). Over this truncated time period, the R-square value for the regression exceeded .99. Then the coefficient estimates for the regression equation along with data for the independent variables from 1948 to 1982 were used to generate predicted values for the IPD for defense purchases from 1948 to 1982. These predicted values were used in constructing **defense** and **defcapital.**

Note: IPD is an abbreviation for implicit price deflator; FTE is an abbreviation for full-time equivalent. All IPDs are fixed at 100 in their base year, 1972.

Sources: All data were provided by CITIBASE (maintained by the Economics Department of Citibank) except **deaths, draft, partynat, soviet,** and the numerators of **officers** and **vet:vote.** Other sources are as follows: **deaths** from *Defense Department Yearly Almanac;* **partynat** from *Book of the States;* the numerator of **vet:vote** from *Statistical Abstract of the United States;* **soviet** from Ward (1984); **officers** from Department of Defense, *Military Manpower Statistics,* July 1984.

154

TABLE 6.5
Results for the Responsive Defense Purchases Equations

Column:	(1)	(2)	(3)	(4)
Equation No.:	6.20	6.23	6.21	6.22
		Dependent Variable		
Independent Variable	defense_t	defcapital_t	milpop_t	milpop_t
partynat_{t-1}	-.017 (.011)	-.010 (.009)		
deaths_t	.00044 (.00110)	.000097 (.000945)		
soviet_{t-1}	-.0017*** (.0002)	-.0013*** (.0002)		
vet:vote_{t-1}	-1.24** (.35)	-.90** (.30)		
defense_t			.14*** (.01)	
defcapital_t				.16*** (.02)
draft_t			-.022 (.013)	-.029* (.013)
$[(\text{relwage}_{t-1})(\text{draft}_t)]$			.022 (.015)	.030 (.015)
Intercept	.46	.34	.02	.02
R^2	.79	.74	.84	.83
n	(33)	(33)	(34)	(34)
Order of AR Process	2	2	1	1

*$p < .05$; **$p < .01$; ***$p < .001$.

Note: All coefficients are unstandardized; standard errors are in parentheses below coefficients. All equations are estimated using pseudo-GLS and assuming an autoregressive (AR) error structure with the order indicated in the last row of this table.

Source: Compiled by the authors.

7

GROWTH IN THE
SCOPE OF GOVERNMENT
TRANSFERS

In the previous two chapters, we develop and test models accounting for three components of postwar government growth: public sector cost growth, and the real change in the scopes of domestic purchases and defense purchases. This chapter completes our disaggregation of government growth by examining both responsive and excessive interpretations of real change in the scope of government transfer payments to individuals.

TWO INTERPRETATIONS OF THE SCOPE
OF GOVERNMENT TRANSFERS

A Responsive Interpretation of Government Transfers

In developing a responsive model of transfers, we must examine external sources of demand for growth, just as we did in the case of the responsive domestic and defense purchases models. However, here we must consider the forces that encourage government to collect revenues and distribute it directly to individuals. We will see that several of the factors proposed as determinants of the scope of purchases are also hypothesized to influence the scope of transfers whereas other determinants are unique to an explanation of transfers.

As noted earlier, Wagner's Law sees much of the growth of the public sector as due to the increasing affluence associated with industrialization. Although in its original form, Wagner's Law seems most relevant for explaining growth in purchases, the income effect Wagner proposed may also be relevant for transfers. Wagner's Law proposes that demand for collective goods will rise as incomes increase. But some have argued that income equity can itself be conceived as a collective good, and one that can be purchased with transfer spending (Due and Friedlander 1977, pp. 98-106; Page 1983). For instance, Thurow (1980) contends that the 1960s brought large increases in transfer spending in the United States because the nation was relatively prosperous; the affluence of the era permitted U.S. citizens to purchase the luxury good of greater income equity through increased transfer payments to the poor. Thus, our responsive government model of transfers includes societal income as an independent variable.

Our earlier analysis of Wagner's Law prompted a consideration of the role of demographic changes in influencing the scope of domestic purchases. Demographics also play an important role in our responsive government transfers model. But the relevant demographic variables are different. When attempting to explain the scope of transfers, we must consider the sizes of groups likely to be highly reliant on government for support. We must be careful when determining the sizes of groups likely to be reliant on government to avoid measuring the size of a group by counting the number of individuals actually receiving government support. If group size were measured in this manner, the hypothesis that group size is related to the scope of government transfers would be nearly tautological. We try to avoid falling into this trap by defining groups in a manner unrelated to the reception of benefits.

Three groups seem especially reliant on government for support: the elderly, the poor, and veterans of the military. With industrialization, there has been a decrease in the traditional sources of assistance for the elderly and the poor: the nuclear and extended families, churches, and other charities. For example, as women participate more extensively in the labor force, the elderly are less frequently cared for in the home, and women have less time available for volunteer work with churches and other charitable organizations. As a result, support for the aged and the poor has become a major obligation of government. So, in an industrialized society, the simple sizes of the poor and elderly populations should influence the scope of government transfers.

The final group whose size should influence the transfers share is veterans. Clearly, veterans are viewed as people who have served their country. Furthermore, many argue that veterans have suffered objective losses that make them deserving of special benefits from government. Of course, some combat veterans sustain crippling injuries during battle. But even those that serve in peacetime are typically at a competitive disadvantage in the labor market when they return to private life. For these reasons, governments should view former military personnel as citizens with a special need for, and claim to, government services.

The responsive government interpretation also suggests that elections should influence the scope of government transfers. Certainly, much has been written about the impact of state electoral competition on redistributive policy; according to Key (1949) and others (for example, Dawson and Robinson 1963; Fry and Winters 1970; Plotnick and Winters 1986), intense interparty competition generates incentives for politicians to be responsive to the needs of have-nots in society.[1] In the present case, however, we do not expect the level of interparty competition, as it is usually conceived, to have a substantial influence on the scope of government transfers. Although the level of party competition may matter in comparative state analyses of transfer spending, the overall level of state party competition in the nation as a whole has remained reasonably stable over the postwar era (Jewell and Olson 1978). And in any case, despite the attention given the influence of party competition on welfare spending in the states, we would expect the federal role to be far more important in determining the scope of government transfers. And at the national level, even though there have been several landslide elections, that these landslides have benefited both parties at different, closely proximate times suggests that the level of party competition was quite robust throughout the entire period. Thus, the range of variation in interparty competitiveness seems much too limited to be able to explain growth in the scope of transfers.

Our review of the electoral competition explanation of government growth in Chapter 3 identified a second aspect of competition, the temporal proximity of the next election, which seems more relevant to the determination of the scope of government transfers. Many studies have found that public officials mold their spending and taxing policies to promote their prospects for reelection (for example, Tufte 1978; Frey and Schneider 1978). We should expect popular policy actions to take place immediately before elections and unpopular actions to occur when elections are as far in the future as possible. Based on this analysis, we should expect government officials to increase the scope of transfers during election years.[2] Moreover, as a result of the entitlement provisions that have existed in most transfer programs during the period of analysis, any increases in transfer benefits adopted during election years should become permanent additions to the transfers budget.

This anticipated electoral effect could be consistent with both the responsive and excessive interpretations. An extreme responsive interpretation might view any transfer benefits given as the outgrowth of legitimate influence by recipient groups in a pluralist democracy. In contrast, an extreme excessive interpretation might see the electoral effect as insidious; in this view, the benefits received by transfer recipients would represent the gains from a selfish alliance between elected officials and recipients to promote their own interests at the public's expense.

If both interpretations of the scope of government transfers predict an electoral effect, how could we determine whether the observation of such an effect would support the responsive or the excessive interpretation? In the ideal world, we would have some standard for judging whether the magnitude of election-year transfer hikes is excessive, that is, more than could be justified based on some objective criterion of need. But, of course, there is no such accepted standard. Nevertheless, there is hope of interpreting the meaning of an electoral effect because we believe the excessive and responsive interpretations generate predictions of somewhat different kinds of electoral effects.

Understanding this difference requires an analysis of how party control of government interacts with the electoral effect in influencing the scope of transfers. Just as our responsive domestic purchases model does, our responsive transfers model hypothesizes that the scope of transfers should be greater during years in which government is controlled by a liberal party than in years in which conservatives are in control. This prediction is based on the differences between traditional liberal and conservative ideologies with regard to the proper role of government. In general, conservatives tend to favor the income distribution generated by the neutral forces of the market (Buchanan 1975; Friedman and Friedman 1980). In contrast, liberals are more likely to view the distribution of income arrived at by the market as less than neutral and to support redistribution through the use of transfer programs.

Similarly, our responsive government model posits that the size of the electoral effect should differ depending on the party in power in the preelection period. The argument is that parties' ideologies limit the actions they are willing to take during election campaigns (Cowart 1978; Tufte 1978). Because the use of transfers for redistribution is more ideologically acceptable to liberals than conservatives, the election-year transfer increases when a liberal party controls government should be greater than those increases that occur when a conservative government is in power. Of course, the incentive to win an election may lead governments dominated by conservatives to increase transfers somewhat. But conservative resistance to employing transfers for redistribution should serve to restrain the magnitude of such increases.

In contrast, our excessive government model does not predict that party control should influence the scope of transfers because the motivations that are thought to prompt public officials to increase transfers are presumed to be equally compelling to both conservatives and liberals. Furthermore, our excessive government interpretation anticipates that any effect an election has on increasing the level of transfers should not depend on the party in power during the campaign period. If politicians are motivated principally by a selfish desire to win elections, and transfer recipients are motivated by a selfish desire to increase their benefits, electoral competition should encourage politicians of both parties to forge the same alliance with interest groups. This argument is consistent with Key's (1949) classic hypothesis that strong interparty competition results in benefits for society's have-nots regardless of which party happens to control government.

The responsive government interpretation also suggests the hypothesis that the sizes of the elderly, the poor, and the veteran populations should interact with party control in their effects on the scope of transfers. Clearly, the tendency to view these groups as especially reliant on government is not found only among liberals. Even conservative President Reagan often alludes to the concept of a government "safety net" for the "truly needy." But liberals' ideological support for (and conservatives' aversion to) transfers as a tool for redistribution and liberals' advocacy for an activist role for government should encourage liberal governments to respond with larger transfer increases than conservative governments when faced with the same increases in the sizes of these groups. Thus, our responsive government model posits that the influence of the sizes of the elderly, the poor, and the veteran populations on the scope of transfers should be more pronounced when government is dominated by a liberal party's members than when it is controlled by conservatives.

Finally, our responsive government interpretation hypothesizes that macroeconomic conditions influence the share of GDP devoted to transfers. Certainly, Peacock and Wiseman's (1961) concentration-displacement explanation calls attention to the role of economic conditions in determining the size of the public sector. They propose that economic crises, such as massive recessions, cause growth in government (see

Chapter 3). But the concentration-displacement explanation is inconsistent with a responsive government interpretation. This is because it suggests that while government grows in response to the needs for increased public sector activity created by a crisis, government fails to shrink when the is over and the need for heightened public sector activity is presumably diminished.

Our proposition that economic conditions affect the scope of government transfers derives instead from the workings of Keynesian macroeconomics. In particular, given the acceptance by policy makers of Keynesian economics since the late 1940s (Lerner 1978; Stein 1978; Lowery 1985), one should expect that the share of total economic activity devoted to transfer payments would increase in periods of recession and decline in periods of economic health. Under Keynesian principles, both automatic stabilizers (for example, changes in the number of individuals eligible for welfare when the unemployment rate changes) and discretionary responses (for example, special extensions of unemployment compensation eligibility periods during economic downturns) can be used to flatten the business cycle. This thinking prompts the responsive government hypothesis that the unemployment rate should be a determinant of the scope of government transfers.

Consequently, we offer the following formalization of the responsive government transfers model:

$$
\begin{aligned}
\text{TRANSFERS}_t = {} & B_0 + B_1\text{UNEMPL}_t + B_2\text{INCOME}_{t-1} \\
& + B_3\text{PARTYNAT}_{t-1} + B_4\text{LIBELEC}_t \\
& + B_5\text{CONELEC}_t + B_6\text{VET:POP}_{t-1} \\
& + B_7\text{OLD:POP}_{t-1} + B_8\text{POOR:POP}_{t-1} \\
& + B_9[(\text{VET:POP}_{t-1})(\text{PARTYNAT}_{t-1})] \\
& + B_{10}[(\text{OLD:POP}_{t-1})(\text{PARTYNAT}_{t-1})] \\
& + B_{11}[(\text{POOR:POP}_{t-1})(\text{PARTYNAT}_{t-1})] + E_t \quad (7.1)
\end{aligned}
$$

The dependent variable, TRANSFERS_t, is the scope of government transfers in year t. UNEMPL denotes the unemployment rate; the current (that is, year t) rate is used because of the immediacy of automatic stabilization responses to shifts in the economy. Two variables were introduced in earlier chapters: INCOME, representing total personal income, and PARTYNAT, an index of the degree of liberal party control of the national government. PARTYNAT ranges from 0 to 1. The coefficients B_1, B_2, and B_3 are expected to be positive.

Our specification of the electoral effect is accomplished with the variables **LIBELEC** and **CONELEC**. When considering the U.S. federal government, it is appropriate to conceptualize party control as a continuous concept ranging from complete control by a conservative party to complete control by a liberal party, as does our variable **PARTYNAT**. But, if party control is to be viewed as a continuous variable, a model that specifies the hypothesis that the size of an electoral effect is linearly dependent on the "value of party control" would require a dummy independent variable for each election during the period of analysis. And if this set of dummy variables were included in equation 7.1 along with the other independent variables, there would be a substantial degrees of freedom problem. Thus, for the purpose of modeling the responsive government electoral effect, we simplify the analysis by viewing party control as dichotomous. In particular, we shall think of dichotomizing **PARTYNAT** at the mean (.5), thereby producing two categories of control: (predominantly) conservative and (predominantly) liberal.

Given this measurement of party control, $LIBELEC_t$ is the number of presidential election years between 1949 and year t when the liberal party is dominant. $CONELEC_t$ denotes the number of election years when the conservatives are dominant. Then, the slope coefficients for these counter variables, **LIBELEC** and **CONELEC**, can be interpreted as the average sizes of the "step changes" in the scope of government transfers occurring in an election year, when a liberal party controls government and when a conservative party controls government, respectively, holding all other variables constant. The expectation is that B_4 and B_5 should both be positive, but that B_4 is greater than B_5, because the responsive model predicts that liberal governments should produce larger election year increases than conservative governments.

VET:POP, **OLD:POP**, and **POOR:POP** denote the share of the total population represented by veterans, the elderly, and the poor, respectively; the coefficients for these three variables should be positive. Although these groups' sizes are hypothesized to have some influence on the scope of transfers regardless of the party in control, our responsive interpretation suggests that their influence becomes stronger as the degree of liberal party control of the national government becomes greater. Thus, we incorporate three multiplicative terms in equation 7.1 to specify the proposition that party control and the group sizes interact in affecting the scope of transfers. The coefficients for all multiplicative terms should be positive.

An Excessive Government Interpretation of Government Transfers

As do our earlier excessive government models, our excessive transfers model suggests that growth in transfers is due primarily to self-interested behavior by government officials. In an earlier comparison of the responsive and excessive interpretations of transfers, we noted that the excessive model foresees an effect of elections on the scope of transfers. More specifically, our excessive model postulates that the election incentive should prompt public officials to increase the scope of transfers during presidential election years and that the entitlement provisions in U.S. transfer programs should lock in these increases for succeeding years.

Our excessive interpretation also leads to the prediction that the sizes of groups have an effect on the scope of government transfers, but for a reason very different from our responsive model. The excessive interpretation focuses on the political pressure that large groups can place on public officials. Groups are presumed to exercise influence through active lobbying, supplemented by the power to reward or punish candidates by controlling the votes of members (Wildavsky 1980; Peltzman 1980; Riker 1980). Certainly, this logic is more convincing when applied to the case of transfers than to that of purchases. Transfer payments provide very tangible benefits to citizens whereas the rewards to the public from purchases are generally more diffuse and less tangible. In essence, the potential for increased transfer payments may provide an incentive sufficient to induce direct political activity to seek the increases. If this were the case, large interest groups may have the votes and other resources necessary to extract large increases in transfer payments.

Olson's (1965) analysis of the logic of collective action suggests that the "free-rider" problem is accentuated as the size of a group increases. This implies that an increase in an interest group's size may lead to a diminution in its lobbying effectiveness. But even if Olson is correct, active lobbying may not be essential for interest groups to be successful in gaining transfer benefits. Elected officials may have sufficient incentive to establish new transfer programs and to boost benefit levels for existing programs even if there are no active efforts by citizens to obtain benefits (Fiorina 1977; 1984). Large transfer payments are still probably welcomed by recipients even if they did not actively seek increases in their benefits. If this were the case, politicians should still reap rewards on election day from increases in the benefit levels for programs serving large groups. As a result, the excessive government model proposes that a group's size is positively related to its success in obtaining transfer benefits. In particular, our model includes the sizes of four groups, each reputed to have substantial voting power: the elderly, veterans, farmers, and the poor.

Furthermore, the excessive government view suggests that the electoral and group effects just described should be interactive. If government officials do lavish transfer benefits on groups with substantial voting power to increase their chances of winning election, it should also be the case that these officials time increases in these benefits to receive maximum electoral advantage. And clearly the most advantageous time is an election year. Thus, our excessive model predicts that the influence of group sizes on the scope of government transfers should be stronger in a presidential election year than in nonelection years.

Finally, the institutional centralization and fiscal illusion hypotheses presented when formulating the excessive domestic purchases model appear equally appropriate when explaining the scope of transfers. If government manipulates the tax system to create a fiscal illusion that pushes voters to demand more from government than would be optimal, some of the resulting revenue may be used to finance transfer programs. Additionally, the reasons presented in Chapter 3 for hypothesizing that the degree of institutional centralization is negatively related to the size of the public sector should apply equally well to the transfers and domestic purchases components of government activity.

These excessive government hypotheses combine to suggest the following model:

$$
\begin{aligned}
\mathrm{TRANSFERS}_t = {} & B_0 + B_1 \mathrm{NUMELEC}_t + B_2 \mathrm{DEBT}_{t-1} + B_3 \mathrm{WHELD}_{t-1} \\
& + B_4 \mathrm{COMPLEX}_{t-1} + B_5 \mathrm{REVCEN}_{t-1} + B_6 \mathrm{AID}_{t-1} \\
& + B_7 \mathrm{VET\!:\!VOTE}_{t-1} + B_8 \mathrm{FARM\!:\!VOTE}_{t-1} \\
& + B_9 \mathrm{OLD\!:\!VOTE}_{t-1} + B_{10} \mathrm{POOR\!:\!VOTE}_{t-1} \\
& + B_{11}[(\mathrm{VET\!:\!VOTE}_{t-1})(\mathrm{ELECTION}_t)] \\
& + B_{12}[(\mathrm{FARM\!:\!VOTE}_{t-1})(\mathrm{ELECTION}_t)] \\
& + B_{13}[(\mathrm{OLD\!:\!VOTE}_{t-1})(\mathrm{ELECTION}_t)] \\
& + B_{14}[(\mathrm{POOR\!:\!VOTE}_{t-1})(\mathrm{ELECTION}_t)] + E_t \qquad (7.2)
\end{aligned}
$$

Several of the variables in this equation appear in models derived earlier. **TRANSFERS** is the scope of government transfers. The fiscal illusion variables are **DEBT**, the ratio of government debt to spending, **WHELD**, the share of government revenues collected by withholding from pay checks, and **COMPLEX**, the degree of complexity of the tax system. The coefficients for all three of these variables are predicted to be positive. The institutional centralization variables are **REVCEN**, the extent to which the tax collection function is controlled by the national government, which should yield a negative slope coefficient, and **AID**, the degree to which government spending is financed through the use of grants-in-aid, which should produce a positive coefficient.

Because the excessive government interpretation attributes the influence of groups to their voting power, the sizes of groups in equation 7.2 are measured as a percentage of the potential electorate. Thus, **VET:VOTE, FARM:VOTE, OLD:VOTE,** and **POOR:VOTE** are the shares of the voting age population accounted for by veterans, farmers, the elderly, and the poor, respectively. **ELECTION** is a dichotomous variable equaling 1 in presidential election years and 0 in nonelection years. It is used in the equation to specify interaction between the occurrence of an election and the strength of group effects. Because the effects of group sizes on the scope of transfers are presumed to be present in nonelection years, but stronger in election years, the coefficients for the four group variables, and for all multiplicative terms are expected to be positive.

The final variable in equation 7.2 is $NUMELEC_t$, a variable included to model the existence of the excessive government electoral effect. It is, in essence, a counter variable. Specifically, it equals the number of presidential elections occurring between 1949 and year t. The slope coefficient for **NUMELEC**, B_1, should be interpreted as the average step change in the scope of government transfers occurring in presidential election years, holding all other variables constant. As such, B_1 should be greater than zero.

TESTING THE MODELS OF THE SCOPE OF GOVERNMENT TRANSFERS

Operationalizing the Models

Both the responsive and excessive interpretations of the scope of government transfers are specified as single-equation models (equations 7.1 and 7.2, respectively). Just as our earlier models, they are tested with time series data from 1948 to 1982. When operationalized, these models take the following form:

Responsive Government Equation

$$
\begin{aligned}
\text{transfers}_t = b_0 &+ b_1\text{unempl}_t + b_2\text{income}_{t-1} + b_3\text{partynat}_{t-1} + b_4\text{demelec}_t \\
&+ b_5\text{repelec}_t + b_6\text{vet:pop}_{t-1} + b_7\text{old:pop}_{t-1} + b_8\text{poor:pop}_{t-1} \\
&+ b_9[(\text{vet:pop}_{t-1})(\text{partynat}_{t-1})] \\
&+ b_{10}[(\text{old:pop}_{t-1})(\text{partynat}_{t-1})] \\
&+ b_{11}[(\text{poor:pop}_{t-1})(\text{partynat}_{t-1})] + e_t
\end{aligned}
\tag{7.3}
$$

Excessive Government Equation

$$
\begin{aligned}
\text{transfers}_t = b_0 &+ b_1\text{numelec}_t + b_2\text{debt}_{t-1} + b_3\text{wheld}_{t-1} + b_4\text{complex}_{t-1} \\
&+ b_5\text{revcen}_{t-1} + b_6\text{aid}_{t-1} + b_7\text{vet:vote}_{t-1} + b_8\text{farm:vote}_{t-1} \\
&+ b_9\text{old:vote}_{t-1} + b_{10}\text{poor:vote}_{t-1} \\
&+ b_{11}[(\text{vet:vote}_{t-1})(\text{election}_t)] \\
&+ b_{12}[(\text{farm:vote}_{t-1})(\text{election}_t)] \\
&+ b_{13}[(\text{old:vote}_{t-1})(\text{election}_t)] \\
&+ b_{14}[(\text{poor:vote}_{t-1})(\text{election}_t)] + e_t
\end{aligned}
\tag{7.4}
$$

Each of the indicators in the two equations is defined in Table 7.1. Several can be recognized from previous chapters. **Income** is used in the test of the responsive domestic purchases model (for example, equation 6.7); the national government party control measure, **partynat**, is an independent variable in the responsive defense purchases model (for example, equation 6.20). The fiscal illusion indicators (**debt, wheld,** and **complex**) and those used to test the institutional centralization hypothesis (**revcen** and **aid**) are used in several excessive government models (for example, equation 6.11). **Vet:vote, farm:vote, old:vote,** and **poor:vote** all measure the size of a group relative to the voting age population. These same four indicators are used in equation 4.5 to test the interest group explanation of government growth.

Several variables have not been used in previous models. The scope of transfers is measured by the real share of GDP represented by transfer payments and is denoted by **transfers. Unempl** is the unemployment rate. **Vet:pop, old:pop,** and **poor:pop** are the indicators used to measure the group size variables in the responsive model; each measures the size of a group as a percentage of the total population. The variable

numelec is the counter variable constructed to reflect the excessive government electoral effect.

Our specification of the responsive government explanation's electoral effect is based on the recognition that the variation in the value of **partynat** in presidential elections during the period of analysis is quite restricted. Indeed, in all presidential election years between 1950 and 1982, **partynat** equals .50 or 1.00. So, two counter variables are employed to specify the responsive electoral effect. **Demelec**$_t$ is the number of presidential elections between 1949 and year t in which **partynat** equals 1, when the liberal (Democratic) party controls the presidency and both houses of Congress. In contrast, **repelec**$_t$ is the number of elections after 1949 and before 1982 when there is split control of the federal government (that is, **partynat** equals .50), such that the Democrats have majorities in both houses of Congress, but the president is Republican. Given these definitions, the coefficient for **repelec** can be interpreted as the expected magnitude of the step change in the scope of government transfers occurring during elections years when there is split control of the national government; **demelec** represents the step change expected during years characterized by Democratic dominance.

Findings for the Government Transfers Models

The Responsive Government Interpretation

The responsive view predicts that all partial slope coefficients in equation 7.3 are positive and additionally that b_4 is greater than b_5. The statistical results relating to our test of equation 7.3 are contained in Table 7.2. But we do not report coefficient estimates for the full version of this equation because it is characterized by so much multicollinearity that the coefficients for it are virtually meaningless. With all 11 independent variables included, for each independent variable except for **unempl** and **vet:pop**, regressing it on the remaining independent variables produces an R-square value exceeding .90; for six of these variables, the R-square is actually greater than .99. Such extreme multicollinearity is not terribly surprising; indeed, it is quite common in models containing several multiplicative terms (Althauser 1971).

We believe the "least of the evils" available to overcome this multicollinearity is to "pull" the product terms from the model, thereby generating the estimates in column 1 of Table 7.2. Although this change diminishes the multicollinearity considerably, it also changes the model; the revised version no longer specifies the hypothesis that the influence of group sizes on the scope of transfers varies with the political party controlling government. Moreover, there is still substantial multicollinearity present in the model of column 1.[3] Therefore, in estimating the coefficients in column 2, we also abandon the assumption that the strength of the electoral effect varies according to party control, by deleting **repelec** and **demelec** in favor of the single variable **numelec** (used in equation 7.4 and defined in Table 7.1). The coefficient for **numelec** should be greater than zero. Finally, because **old:pop** and **poor:pop** are highly correlated over the postwar period, we also estimate coefficients for two other models in which just **old:pop** or **poor:pop** is included. These results are reported in columns 3 and 4.

The results in Table 7.2 lend clear support to several hypotheses. First, the unemployment rate seems to affect the scope of government transfers in the manner predicted by the responsive interpretation. The positive and significant coefficient for **unempl** in all versions of equation 7.3 suggests that increases in unemployment prompt increases in the transfers share of GDP. The variable **income** also produced positive and statistically significant coefficients in all versions of the model. Consistent with the logic of Wagner's Law, increases in societal personal income seem to lead to increases in the scope of government transfers.

Moreover, party control seems to have the anticipated effect on the scope of transfers. Three of the four models reported in Table 7.2 yield statistically significant positive coefficients for **partynat**, and the fourth produces a parameter estimate missing significance at the .05 level by just "a hair." These results indicate that governments controlled by the liberal party produce a higher transfers share of GDP than governments subject to more conservative party control.

Although party control seems to have the hypothesized effect, there is no indication of the presence of an electoral effect of the type predicted by the responsive government interpretation. The results for the only equation that allows the electoral effect to vary depending on the nature of party control are in column 1. Here, the coefficient for **repelec** is positive as hypothesized. But the parameter for **demelec** is inconsistent with the responsive government prediction. Indeed, not only does it fail to be greater than that for **repelec**; the coefficient for **demelec** is slightly negative. Therefore, if there is a party-control-determined electoral effect, equations, which restrict any electoral effect to be independent of the the step change in the scope of transfers in years of liberal party government control is actually somewhat downward. The other party in control, generate inconsistent results. The coefficient for **numelec** is positive in two models (indicating a slight election year step increase), but negative in the third (suggesting a small decrease). Accordingly, if an electoral effect exists, it is not a strong one and is not one consistent with the prediction of the responsive government interpretation.

The findings about the group size hypotheses are also mixed. The size of the veteran population proves to be positively related to the scope of government transfers, as predicted. Although **vet:pop**'s coefficient is not statistically significant at the .05 level in any of the four models, it is significant at the .10 level in three equations. But the size of the poor population seems to be virtually unrelated to the scope of transfers; the parameter for **poor:pop** fluctuates from weakly positive to weakly negative across the multiple tests. Finally, the relationship between the size of the elderly population (**old:pop**) and the transfers share of GDP is actually negative. Certainly of the three groups, veterans have been the most effectively mobilized for political action during the postwar era, and this may account for the relative success of **vet:pop** in generating a positive coefficient. But the responsive government interpretation's prediction of group size effects is based on the presumption that these three groups are seen as especially reliant on government for support. If it is the superior mobilization by veterans that is responsible for the positive coefficient for **vet:pop**, that positive value should not be viewed as supporting the responsive interpretation. Thus it is unwise to claim any substantial support for the group effect component of the responsive government model.

The Excessive Government Interpretation

The multicollinearity accompanying estimation of the excessive government transfers model is even more extreme than that attending the responsive model. For ten of the independent variables (including all the multiplicative terms), regressing it on the remaining ones generates an R-square value greater than .99. And **debt** is the only independent variable that when regressed on the rest, produces an R-square value under .90. But as with the responsive model, the least objectionable course for overcoming the crippling multicollinearity is to delete the model's multiplicative terms. This change forces an assumption that the magnitudes of the effects of group sizes on the transfers share of GDP do not depend on whether it is an election year. The results for this modified equation are reported in column 1 of Table 7.3.

Moreover, the same set of fiscal illusion and institutional centralization variables that produce strong multicollinearity in the excessive government domestic purchases model is in the transfers model too. Thus, we employ the same strategy for estimation that we used earlier. In particular, we estimate the parameters of models in which one of **wheld** and **complex**, and one of **revcen** and **aid** are deleted. The results for these four equations are in columns 2 through 5 of Table 7.3. Three of the four group variables, **farm:vote, old:vote**, and **poor:vote**, are also highly collinear. So we estimated variations of equation 7.3 that contained **vet:vote** and only one of the other group variables (see columns 6 through 8). Lastly, the missing data for **complex** and **wheld** (see Table 7.1), reduce the sample size for all the above tests (n = 23 or 24); we can expand our degrees of freedom considerably (to n = 34) by removing these two variables. Column 9 presents the results for this restricted model.

Several of the excessive government hypotheses receive statistical support. First, the institutional centralization proposition is confirmed. There is consistent evidence that increases in reliance on intergovernmental fiscal aid and greater decentralization of the revenue collection function are associated with expansion of the scope of transfers. The results of the most complete model (column 1 of Table 7.3) are deceptive concerning the strength of these relationships; although the coefficients for **revcen** and **aid** both have their predicted sign (in spite of the large negative correlation between the two variables), neither is statistically significant. But when multicollinearity is diminished by excluding one of these variables, the relationship of institutional centralization to the transfers share appears stronger. The parameter for **revcen** is uniformly negative in the restricted models, and in five of the six models, it is significant at the .05 level. The indicator **aid** is alone in two models; and although **aid**'s coefficient is not significant in either model, it is of moderate strength in both cases.

Second, there is also substantial evidence consistent with the fiscal illusion proposition. The strongest support exists for the withholding illusion. The coefficient for **wheld** is strongly positive in all models, suggesting that greater reliance on tax withholding is associated with the expansion of transfers. Similarly, the findings appear to give support for the hypothesis that tax system complexity is positively related to the scope of government transfers. The negative coefficient for **complex** in column 1 appears to be an artifact of the strong correlation between **complex** and **wheld** because both versions of the excessive transfers model excluding **wheld** yield a strong positive coefficient for **complex.** The support for the hypothesized debt-financing illusion is much weaker. Clearly, most of the versions of equation 7.4 tested produce the predicted positive coefficient for **debt.** But the strengths of these coefficients vary from strong to quite weak. And in the equation taking advantage of the full data set (column 9), the parameter for debt is negative. However, despite the mixed results concerning the debt illusion, the stronger evidence for the withholding and tax system complexity arguments suggests general support for the fiscal illusion proposition as applied to government transfers.

Third, there is some support for the type of electoral effect anticipated by the excessive government perspective. The coefficient estimate for **numelec** is positive across all tests of the model, and in the version having the greatest degrees of freedom (see column 9), the coefficient is statistically significant. But we must be cautious in claiming support for the electoral effect hypothesis, for in all other equations, the coefficient for **numelec** is very weak. So, it seems that if elections do encourage public officials to increase the scope of transfers, the resulting increases are fairly small.

The remaining hypothesis of the excessive government interpretation — concerning the influence of interest group sizes — also receives only limited empirical support. Severe multicollinearity makes it impossible to test the proposition that the effects of group sizes on the scope of transfers are greater in an election year than in other years. But the results are consistent with the proposition that the transfers share grows along with the voting power of several groups. This is clearly true for farmers. The coefficient for **farm:vote** is uniformly positive in all versions of equation 7.4 and is statistically significant when other group variables are removed to reduce multicollinearity (see column 6).

For each of the other three groups — the elderly, the poor, and veterans — most of the findings in Table 7.3 support the voting power hypothesis. But in each case, the statistical evidence is weaker and less consistent. For example, the coefficient for the size of the veterans voting block (**vet:vote**) is positive in seven of the nine equations tested, but none of the positive coefficients come close to statistical significance, not even those in the restricted equations designed to minimize multicollinearity. Similarly, the coefficient for the voting power of the elderly (**old:vote**) is positive in five of seven equations but is statistically significant only in an equation in which it is negative in value. Finally, although the coefficient for the size of the poor population (**poor:vote**) is positive and significant in the equation characterized by the least multicollinearity (see column 8), it is near zero or even negative in the remaining versions. Thus, although there is some support for the excessive government claim that elected officials reward members of groups controlling a large number of votes with transfer benefits, there is no evidence that the rewards are substantial in magnitude.

Conclusion

Both competing interpretations of growth in the scope of transfers — responsive and excessive — receive considerable empirical support from our statistical analyses. Consonant with the responsive government view, the scope of transfers appears to respond to changes in the unemployment rate and to increases in the demand for transfers that accompany greater economic affluence. Also, if election results can be assumed to reflect public attitudes about the size of government, the finding that governments dominated by the liberal party oversee greater transfers shares than more conservative governments represents further evidence that the scope of transfers is responsive to fluctuations in the level of public demand. Our results, however, are consistent with the excessive government assertion that more centralized governments are more capable of controlling the expansionist tendencies inherent in governments. They also conform to the prediction by excessive government theorists that governments seek to fashion fiscal illusions that facilitate the expansion of government. Specifically, we find evidence of fiscal illusions created by withholding taxes from pay checks and by adopting a highly complex tax structure relying on numerous sources of revenue.

If there is a difference in the amount of support garnered by the two competing explanations of transfers growth, it centers in the results concerning the influence of elections and group sizes on the scope of transfers. Although there is no support for the kind of electoral effect envisioned by the responsive government view, there is some evidence of at least a slight electoral effect consistent with the excessive interpretation. However, we can not differentiate the degrees of support for the two different types of electoral effects with great confidence because multicollinearity prevented us from testing for the responsive electoral effect as it was originally specified. Similarly, the support for the group voting power hypothesis of the excessive model is slightly stronger than that for the responsive government group size proposition. But again, we can not make too much of this difference because, in this case, the excessive government proposition — predicting interaction between group voting power and the presence of elections — was not testable in its full form because of excessive multicollinearity.

In conclusion, both the responsive government interpretation and the excessive interpretation receive substantial support from our empirical analyses. If either can be claimed to receive more support, it would have to be the excessive government view. But the more appropriate conclusion is that our empirical results do not allow us to designate either of the explanations as clearly superior.

NOTES

1.   For elaboration on the logic of this argument, see the discussion of the electoral competition explanation in Chapter 3.

2.   Although elections for some national, state, or local elections occur every year, if elections prompt increases in transfers, the most dramatic increases should occur in presidential election years. This is because in such years, all members of the House of Representatives, one-third of U.S. senators, and a significant number of state and local officials also face election. Consequently, in this chapter, we assume elections take place only once every four years.

3.   When **demelec, repelec, income, old:pop,** or **poor:pop** is regressed on the rest of the independent variables in the model of Table 7.2, column 1, the R-square value is greater than .95.

TABLE 7.1
Description of Indicators Used to Test the Models of the Scope of Government Transfers

Variable	Indicator
aid	Federal and state grants-in-aid to state and/or local governments as a percentage of total federal, state and local expenditures
complex	Herfindahl Index of Revenue Concentration (see Wagner 1976, p. 55) based on eight revenue sources: corporate profits tax, business nontax revenue, customs revenue, estate gift tax, excise tax, income tax, social insurance contributions, and indirect business tax (data only available for period 1959 to 1982)
debt	[Federal, state and local government expenditures minus federal, state and local receipts] as a percentage of [total federal, state and local government expenditures]
demelec	Number of presidential elections between 1949 and the year of measurement when the Democratic party controls both houses of Congress and the president is a Democrat
election	Dichotomous variable which equals 1 during the year of a presidential election, and 0 otherwise
farm:vote	Number of farmers as a percentage of the voting age (i.e., 20 years or older) population
income	Total personal income in billions of dollars divided by IPD for national income
numelec	Number of presidential elections between 1949 and the year of measurement
old:pop	Number of people older than age 64 as a percentage of the total population
old:vote	Number of people older than age 64 as a percentage of the voting age (i.e., 20 years or older) population
partynat	$((H / 4) + (S / 4) + (P / 2))$, where H (or S) equals 1 when the majority party in the United States House (or Senate) is the Democrats, and 0 otherwise; and P equals 1 if the United States president is a Democrat, and 0 otherwise

Table 7.1, Continued

poor:pop	Number of persons below the Poverty Line as a percentage of the total population. For 1953 to 1983, actual data on the number below the Poverty Line are employed. The pre-1959 data are estimated based on a regression of the number of persons below the Poverty Line on the number of recipients of AFDC, the number receiving unemployment compensation, and the number of OAA recipients
poor:vote	Number of persons below the Poverty Line as a percentage of the voting age (i.e., 20 years or older) population [see definition of **poor:pop** for more detail]
repelec	Number of presidential elections between 1949 and the year of measurement when the Democratic party controls both houses of Congress and the president is a Republican
revcen	[Federal government receipts] as a percentage of [total federal, state and local government receipts excluding grants-in-aid]
transfers	Ratio of [total government expenditures for transfer programs divided by IPD for personal consumption expenditures] to [GDP divided by IPD for GDP]
unempl	The unemployment rate
vet:pop	Number of veterans as a percentage of the total population
vet:vote	Number of military veterans as a percentage of the voting-age (i.e., 20 years or older) population
wheld	[Government receipts from social insurance contributions and federal, state and local income taxes] as a percentage of [total federal, state and local government receipts excluding grants-in-aid] (data only available for period 1958 to 1982)

Note: IPD is an abbreviation for implicit price deflator; FTE is an abbreviation for full-time equivalent. All IPDs are fixed at 100 in their base year, 1972.

Sources: All data were provided by CITIBASE (maintained by the Economics Department of Citibank) except **demelec, election, numelec, partynat, poor:pop** (pre-1959), **poor:vote** (pre-1959), **repelec, unempl, vet:pop,** and **vet:vote**. Other sources are the number of veterans component of **vet:pop** and **vet:vote**, and the poverty line, AFDC, unemployment compensation, and OAA data used to estimate pre-1959 values of **poor:pop** and **poor:vote** from *Statistical Abstract of the United States*; **partynat** from *Book of the States*; **unempl** from U.S. Department of Labor, *Handbook of Labor Statistics*.

TABLE 7.2
Results for Responsive Government Transfers Equation 7.3

Column:	(1)	(2)	(3)	(4)
	Dependent Variable			
Independent Variable	transfers$_t$	transfers$_t$	transfers$_t$	transfers$_t$
unempl$_t$	.61*** (.06)	.69*** (.07)	.71*** (.06)	.54*** (.09)
income$_{t-1}$	.00016** (.000012)	.00014*** (.000013)	.00014*** (.00001)	.000088*** (.000018)
partynat$_{t-1}$	.0050* (.0024)	.0082** (.0026)	.0085** (.0025)	.0068 (.0036)
demelec$_t$	-.0018 (.0020)			
repelec$_t$	.0050* (.0020)			
numelec$_t$		.0016 (.0020)	.00083 (.00158)	-.0033 (.0020)
vet:pop$_{t-1}$	.25 (.20)	.44 (.22)	.42 (.22)	.59 (.30)
old:pop$_{t-1}$	-3.1*** (.4)	-2.6*** (.5)	-2.49*** (.4)	
poor:pop$_{t-1}$	-.016 (.036)	.025 (.043)		-.017 (.059)
Intercept	.17	.10	.10	-.09
R^2	.99	.99	.99	.95
n	(34)	(34)	(34)	(34)
Order of AR Process	OLS	OLS	OLS	1

*p < .05; **p < .01; ***p < .001.

Note: All coefficients are unstandardized; standard errors are in parentheses below coefficients. Most equations are estimated with ordinary least squares (OLS) regression; one is estimated using pseudo-GLS and assuming an autoregressive (AR) error structure with order 1 as indicated in the last row of this table.

Source: Compiled by the authors.

TABLE 7.3
Results for Excessive Government Transfers Equation 7.4

Column:	(1)	(2)	(3)	(4)	(5)	(6)	(7)	(8)	(9)
					Dependent Variable				
Independent Variable	$transfers_t$	$transfers_t$	$transfers_t$	$transfers_t$	$transfers_t$	$transfers_t$	$transfers_t$	$transfers_t$	$transfers_t$
$numelec_t$	.0010	.0019	.00073	.0038	.00094	.0031	.0019	.0012	.012**
	(.0047)	(.0032)	(.00431)	(.0039)	(.00482)	(.0023)	(.0026)	(.0023)	(.003)
$debt_{t-1}$	.044	.031	.090*	.046	.095	.023	-.017	.013	-.026
	(.060)	(.039)	(.037)	(.054)	(.046)	(.032)	(.042)	(.035)	(.028)
$wheld_{t-1}$	.0056	.0051***	.0047***			.0049***	.0041***	.0050***	
	(.0028)	(.0009)	(.0011)			(.0008)	(.0007)	(.0009)	
$complex_{t-1}$	-.045			.85**	.87**				
	(.465)			(.22)	(.22)				
$revcen_{t-1}$	-.32	-.33*		-.19		-.33**	-.33*	-.40**	-.34**
	(.20)	(.11)		(.14)		(.09)	(.12)	(.11)	(.09)
aid_{t-1}	.072		.41		.37				
	(.364)		(.25)		(.29)				
$vet:vote_{t-1}$	.32	.30	.56	.34	.56	.18	-.29	.20	-.45
	(.39)	(.31)	(.34)	(.40)	(.37)	(.22)	(.21)	(.25)	(.27)
$farm:vote_{t-1}$	2.3	2.8	2.3	3.8	2.7	2.8**			.56
	(2.5)	(1.7)	(2.3)	(2.2)	(2.7)	(.9)			(2.33)
$old:vote_{t-1}$	.34	.51	1.0	1.6	1.9		-.79		-1.1*
	(1.33)	(.90)	(1.0)	(1.3)	(1.3)		(.86)		(.42)
$poor:vote_{t-1}$	.083	.036	.049	-.19	-.099			.19*	-.0003
	(.213)	(.139)	(.186)	(.16)	(.206)			(.08)	(.1516)
Intercept	-.14	-.14	-.49	-.43	-.66	-.02	.28	.02	.50
R^2	.97	.97	.96	.96	.96	.97	.96	.97	.92
n	(23)	(24)	(24)	(23)	(23)	(24)	(24)	(24)	(34)
Order of AR Process	OLS	OLS	OLS	OLS	OLS	OLS	2	OLS	OLS

*p < .05; **p < .01; ***p < .001.

Note: All coefficients are unstandardized; standard errors are in parentheses below coefficients. Most equations are estimated with ordinary least squares (OLS) regression; one is estimated using pseudo-GLS and assuming an autoregressive (AR) error structure with order 2 as indicated in the last row of this table.

Source: Compiled by the authors.

IV

TOWARD A GREATER UNDERSTANDING OF GOVERNMENT GROWTH

8

GOVERNMENT GROWTH: CONCLUSIONS AND IMPLICATIONS

INTRODUCTION

This book represents a fundamental change in the nature of research on public sector growth. Our results confirm that much can be learned about the causes of government growth by disaggregating the concept government size. More specifically, differentiating between real growth and cost growth, and then further discriminating the real scope of government transfers from the real scope of domestic purchases, which in turn can be differentiated from the scope of defense purchases, has allowed us to explain quite well much of the change in the size of government that has taken place during the postwar period. Furthermore, our results shed some light on the merits of the two dominant competing perspectives on the causes of public sector growth: the responsive and excessive interpretations.

In this final chapter, we summarize and interpret the empirical results of the last three chapters and discuss the limitations of our analyses. We suggest several directions for refining our study of the process of public sector expansion. And finally, we return to the important policy issues raised in Chapter 1 to determine what implications our empirical findings may have on the debate about appropriate policies for dealing with government growth.

Before summarizing the specific findings of Part III, we should review the conclusions of the analyses from Parts I and II of this book. The results of these earlier analyses identified the problems with the traditional approach to the study of government growth that motivated our research approach in Part III. The central conclusion of Part I concerned measurement. Put simply, we found that how you measure the size of government makes a big difference. Growth rates in the postwar era are radically different depending on whether the size of government is measured in constant- or current-dollar terms. Furthermore, the patterns of change in the size of different components of government activity — transfer payments to individuals, purchases of domestic goods and services, and purchases of goods and services for national defense — are strikingly different.

Part II began with a review of a set of single-factor explanations that have dominated research on government growth. We then tested these explanations in the traditional manner, using current-dollar measures for variables. These empirical tests were conducted even though it was clear that such current-dollar measures are inappropriate given the theoretical focus of the single-factor models, the explanation of real growth in the scope of government. Our results were in concert with the general pattern of support for these explanations in the literature; we found that most of the models receive at least some empirical support when tested with current-dollar measures. But then we retested the very same explanations using constant-dollar (or real) measures, and the empirical support for the explanations virtually disappeared. This led us to believe that the body of empirical support for the single-factor explanations of government growth was fundamentally flawed. Indeed, the results of the empirical analysis in Part II of this book made it evident that we could no longer expect the single-factor explanations that have for so long dominated the study of public sector growth to serve as a solid foundation for future research.

We were convinced on both theoretical and empirical grounds that two features of the research approach of Part II were responsible for the failure of the single-factor explanations to account for public sector growth: the single factor nature of the explanations and the high level of aggregation of the dependent variable, the size of government. Thus, part of our task in Part III was to refocus attention away from the size of the public sector as an aggregate and toward four components of this aggregate: the cost of public sector goods and services relative to those in the economy as a whole and changes in the real scopes of government activity in three areas: transfer payments, domestic purchases, and defense purchases. The other part of our task was to develop accounts of these four components that move beyond the traditional single-factor models and thus offer a more realistic hope for explanatory success. We used two dominant theoretical orientations — the excessive and responsive interpretations — to guide the development of our explanations. For this reason, our empirical results have implications for important policy issues associated with recent efforts to constrain growth in the size of government.

SUMMARY OF EMPIRICAL FINDINGS

Given the empirical results of Part III, what conclusions can we draw about the relative merits of the two basic perspectives on the reasons for public sector growth: the responsive and excessive interpretations? Does the public sector expand — as the responsive view presumes — principally as a response to changes in the public's preferences and in economic and social conditions that affect the public's level of demand for government activity? Or does government grow — as the excessive interpretation proposes — primarily as a result of the selfish behavior of public officials and demands for expansion internal to government?

Overall, the responsive government perspective finds more support from our empirical analyses than the excessive interpretation. This pattern, however, is not highly consistent across the four components of government growth. The difference between the support provided the two perspectives is sharpest for the cost growth component. The excessive government interpretation, which attributes growth in the cost of government (relative to costs in the economy at large) to the voting power of public sector employees, receives virtually no empirical support. In contrast, the responsive model derived from the analyses of Beck and Baumol receives substantial support. It appears that the relative cost of providing government goods and services has grown not because of the self-serving behavior of government employees, but instead because of the basic character of government goods and services. Cost growth seems to arise from the high labor intensiveness of traditional public sector activities, along with government's objective need to match wage increases in the private sector to attract and keep employees. The superiority of the responsive government interpretation in explaining cost growth is quite important, given the finding in Chapter 2 that cost growth accounts for such a large share of the total growth in government measured in current-dollar terms.

The responsive government interpretation also proves to offer a much better explanation of the scope of domestic purchases than the excessive view. A model viewing the scope of domestic purchases as responsive to changes in income and social demographics that influence the demand for government services accounts quite well for the change in the scope of domestic purchases over the postwar period. Indeed, the only responsive government hypothesis that fails to be confirmed by our empirical analysis is the party control proposition. In contrast, nearly all the hypotheses derived form the excessive government interpretation must be rejected.

The results concerning the scope of transfers are more ambiguous. Again, the responsive interpretation receives much support. There is evidence that changes in economic conditions and societal affluence determine the level of demand for transfers and, ultimately, the scope of government transfers. Furthermore, to the extent that election outcomes signal changes in public attitudes about government spending, the transfers share seems to be influenced by shifts in public preferences. But there is also empirical support for major elements of the excessive government model of transfers growth. The statistical evidence is consistent with the proposition that public officials create fiscal illusions that allow them to overtax citizens and with the hypothesis that decentralization of the taxing and spending functions promotes government expansion.

In direct contrast, neither interpretation comes close to providing an adequate account of changes in the scope of defense purchases in the postwar era. If one were to seek some solace by identifying support for certain elements of these interpretations, that solace would have to come from the responsive government model. None of the hypotheses generated from the excessive government perspective received support. But some responsive hypotheses were confirmed. For example, there is some evidence that party control influences the scope of defense purchases. On balance, however, the limited pockets of support for the responsive interpretation do not change the fundamental conclusion that there is little support for either interpretation. Most of the logic underlying our explanations of public sector growth, however, is derived from a literature that has, for the most part, ignored defense spending. Thus, if, before our empirical analysis, we had to guess which component of government growth would receive the least support from our models, that guess would probably have been defense purchases.

In conclusion, the responsive government interpretation has considerable power in explaining three of the components of public sector growth: cost growth and real growth in the scopes of domestic purchases and transfer payments to individuals. In contrast, the excessive view fails to shed any light on cost growth or real growth in the scope of purchases. It serves a useful explanatory role only with respect to real transfers growth. On balance, then, the responsive government interpretation seems to represent a superior explanation of public sector growth.

The lack of uniformity in the support found for the various models suggests that our strategy of disaggregation has been fruitful. For example, the responsive government party control hypothesis draws some support from the empirical analyses with transfers and defense purchases but not from those with domestic purchases. Perhaps this has significant substantive implications in confirming the view that the ideological differences between the two parties are stronger on defense issues and redistributive issues involving transfer programs than on decisions about domestic purchases. But the methodological lesson is quite important as well. Consistent with the responsive government perspective our indicator of party control is positively related to the scope of transfers but negatively related to the scope of defense purchases. Moreover, party control seems unrelated to domestic purchases. Such variation in the relationship between party control and the size of the public sector across different types of government activity is lost when all government activity is aggregated together and research is conducted on the determinants of the overall size of government.[1] When all government expenditures are considered together, as has been the standard practice in the literature on government growth, so much may be hidden that we lose the ability to confirm or disconfirm propositions.

Although our findings point to the overall superiority of the responsive interpretation of government growth, we must be careful not to make too strong a point about this superiority. Having disaggregated government growth into components, it is no longer necessary to crown one interpretation as superior for all components. And we believe we should not mask the success of the excessive government explanation of the scope of government transfers by simply issuing a blanket verdict that the responsive view receives more empirical support. Indeed, we believe the recognition that the excessive interpretation can be useful in explaining transfers growth but not purchases growth gives us substantial insight about the limits of that interpretation. On a very general level, there are two distinct versions of the excessive interpretation. The more extreme ascribes government growth to internally generated demands growing from the self-serving behavior of public employees (for example, Goetz 1977; Buchanan and Tullock 1977). The other sees growth as arising from external demands for expansion of government activity interacting with the incentives of elected and nonelected officials to heed these demands (Key 1949; Grodzins 1960; Wildavsky 1980).

Our results suggest that, to the extent that the excessive interpretation is accurate, it is the latter, or less extreme, version that is operative. The finding that the excessive government interpretation fails to explain the expansion of purchases but appears to account well for growth in transfers suggests that public sector growth probably is not a result of the single-minded pursuit of self-interest by government employees. For instance, the support for the fiscal illusion hypothesis with respect to transfers, and the absence of support for it in the case of (domestic and defense) purchases, suggests that if fiscal illusions are used to generate excessive revenues, these revenues are used primarily to finance increased transfer spending. But if sheer employee self-interest were responsible for government expansion, it does not make sense that the excessive revenues would be used to support transfer increases instead of additional purchases because purchases offer government exployees much more tangible rewards.

The limitation of the success of the excessive interpretation to the transfers arena suggests that if the excessive view is correct, most of the demand for expansion must be attributed not to public employees, but to external groups seeking government benefits because interest groups clearly have an incentive to seek transfers rather than purchases. Consequently, to the extent that the excessive government interpretation is correct, it is, in effect, a somewhat responsive form of the interpretation that is so. Of course, if there are strong incentives that virtually force government officials to respond to the selfish interests of groups, and if they react by enacting transfer benefits that require excessive spending, such responsiveness could not be termed healthy. Our empirical support for the responsive interpretation dos not permit us to reject the counterhypothesis that when government responds to public demands (as our evidence suggests they do), it overresponds. Of course, it is impossible to ever reject this counterproposition unless, first, agreement is reached on a normative standard defining an appropriate level of response to external demands. In the absence of such agreement, judgments about the relative support for the excessive and responsive interpretations must be based on empirical analyses of the kind presented in this book. And our analysis casts much doubt on the validity of especially an extreme version of the excessive interpretation that attributes government growth primarily to the actions of self-interested public employees.

EXTENDING THE ANALYSIS

In the case of the transfers share — where both the responsive and excessive interpretations receive empirical support — it is tempting to combine components of both views into a single comprehensive model of public sector growth. Certainly, there is a strong likelihood that the true process by which the scope of government is determined reflects features of both the responsive and excessive interpretations. But data limitations would represent an almost insurmountable hurdle against efforts at a synthesis of two interpretations.

Severe multicollinearity has clearly interfered with our ability to test the separate specifications of the excessive and responsive interpretations of government growth. In several situations in this book, we are forced to abandon a well-specified model in favor of a misspecified model in an effort to confront virtually crippling collinearity. Thus, we must admit that we have not fully tested even the models we have already developed. And this collinearity problem would only be exacerbated if we sought to develop more comprehensive models based on elements of both the responsive and excessive government views. Clearly, with annual data from a period as limited as the postwar era, we are limited in the use of econometric analysis to evaluate models as complex as, or more complex than, those developed here.

To a large degree, we believe this collinearity problem is inherent in research about government growth. It is now well understood that inferences based on cross-sectional analysis about the determinants of a dependent variable, the values of which are actually generated from a dynamic process, can be quite misleading (Brunner and Leipelt 1972; Gray 1976). And clearly values for the size of government are generated out of a longitudinal process. Although moving to cross-national analysis would certainly lessen the collinearity problem, the substantive results about the causes of government growth coming from such analysis would have little utility.

This leaves only two courses of action available for alleviating the multicollinearity problem. First, as some have done, we could extend the analysis back in time (for example, Lewis-Beck and Rice 1984). We have resisted such a course because it is very unlikely that indicators of the kind employed here can be validly compared over extended periods of time (Margolis 1981). Alternatively, and we believe more fruitfully, time-series analysis can be extended to other nations. Although similar collinearity problems are likely to exist in data for other nations as well, the empirical collinearity between hypothesized determinants may be somewhat less severe in some cases.

If one avenue for theoretical advance stands out as most critical, we believe it is the need to consider the relationships among the various components of government growth we have considered. To this point, we have assumed that the growth processes for transfers, domestic purchases, and defense purchases operate independently of each other. But this assumption of independence lacks plausibility. Indeed, there is an extensive literature investigating the extent to which tradeoffs are made between different categories of public expenditure when budgetary decisions are made (Domke, Eichenberg, and Kelleher 1983; Caputo 1975; Wilensky 1978; Russett 1969). Theoretical elaboration of the relationships among growth in the scopes of transfers, domestic purchases, and defense purchases would be an important step in the development of a government growth research program.

The Policy Context of Government Growth

A number of important normative and policy issues associated with the problem of government growth were raised in Chapter 1. As discussed in that chapter, the new conservative critique of big government offers not only an assessment of the causes of government growth, but also an analysis of the consequences of big government and a menu of policy solutions to restrain public sector growth. The analyses presented in Part III of this book have several important implications for evaluating these issues.

First, if the responsive government interpretation is correct, it is not at all clear that the size of public sector needs restraining. If government grows principally in response to increased demand for its services, the growth may be perfectly healthy. Indeed, if growth were not occurring, this would suggest a lack of responsiveness to citizen demands for expansion.

Second, the finding of Chapter 2 that the lion's share of total growth in government over the postwar era (measured in nominal dollars) is due to cost growth, and not to increases in the real scope of government activity, further undercuts the claim that expansion of the public sector is a major threat to freedom. The assertion of a loss of freedom is a claim against big, active government, not expensive government. And cost growth — growth of the cost of government relative to costs in the economy at large — indicates that we are paying more for what government does, not that government is doing more. The finding that the real share of GDP devoted to government has grown only slightly during the postwar period offers no evidence that the scope of government was not too large at the beginning of the period. The question of whether government is absolutely too large or too small is one that cannot be answered with the kinds of analyses presented here. But these same analyses do suggest that the relative amount of real activity conducted in the public and private sectors has not changed a great deal over the postwar era. If there was not a significant freedom problem in 1950, probably neither is there one now.

Even if cost growth does not entail a loss of liberty, it still necessitates ever higher taxes. Thus, the problem of more expensive government cannot be dismissed as trivial. And given the support we find for the responsive government interpretation of cost growth based on the Beck/Baumol model, it is not one that will be easily solved. It certainly will not be solved by the kinds of reforms proposed by the conservative critique of big government.

This observation is the third major implication of our study. Our empirical results offer support for the responsive interpretation for three of the components of government expansion — cost growth and growth in the scopes of transfers and domestic purchases. The common element underlying these three responsive explanations is the assumption that the causes of public sector expansion lie in objective social and economic conditions, not in the narrow selfish interests of government officials. But the policy proposals of the conservative critique of big government do not address these conditions. Instead, they involve constraining government growth through tax limits and fiscal caps. Such steps, obviously, can do nothing about the inherent productivity differential between the public and private sectors or the changing age structure of the population that creates demands for more classrooms because there are more students. Indeed, such policy solutions could cripple our ability to respond to many of these problems.

We would not argue on the basis of the evidence presented here that the responsive account of the growth of government is the final answer to the question of why government grows. For reasons we have already discussed in this chapter, the question remains open. But just as clearly, our findings demonstrate that the excessive government interpretation provides a very poor account of most of the components of public sector expansion. Therefore, we should be very hesitant to adopt institutional reforms that are dependent on the presumed validity of that account.

NOTE

1. Note, for example, the lack of empirical support for the party control explanation in Chapter 4 (see equation 4.10 and Table 4.3).

BIBLIOGRAPHY

Aberbach, J. D., and A. Rockman. 1976. "Clashing Beliefs within the Executive Branch." *American Political Science Review,* 70 (June): 456–68.

Abizadeh, S., and J. Gray. 1985. "Wagner's Law: A Pooled Time Series, Cross-Section Comparison." *National Tax Journal,* 38 (June): 209–18.

Alt, J. E., and K. A. Chrystal. 1983. *Political Economics.* Berkeley, Calif.: University of California Press.

Althauser, R. R. 1971. "Multicollinearity in Non-Additive Regression Models." In *Causal Models in the Social Sciences,* edited by H. M. Blalock, Jr. Chicago: Aldine.

Anton, T. J. 1983. "The Regional Distribution of Federal Expenditures. *National Tax Journal* 36 (December): 429-42.

Arabellera, J. W., and R. P. Labrie. 1982. "Budgeting for Defense: The Original Reagan Five-Year Plan." In *The Federal Budget: Economics and Politics,* edited by M. J. Boskin and A. Wildavsky, pp. 203–34, San Francisco: Institute for Contemporary Studies.

Aranson, P. H., and P. C. Ordeshook. 1981. "Alternative Theories of the Growth of Government and Their Implications for Constitutional Tax and Spending Limits." In *Tax and Spending Limitations,* edited by H. Ladd and T. N. Tideman, pp. 191–222. Washington, D.C.: The Urban Institute.

Arnold, D. 1979. *Congress and the Bureaucracy.* New Haven, Conn.: Yale University Press.

____. 1978. "Legislatures, Overspending, and Government Growth." Paper presented at the Conference on the Causes and Consequences of Public Sector Growth, Dorado Beach, Puerto Rico, November.

Bartlett, R. 1973. *Economic Foundations of Political Power.* New York: The Free Press.

Baumol, W. J. 1967. "Macroeconomics of Unbalanced Growth: The Anatomy of the Urban Crisis." *American Economic Review,* 57 (June): 415–26.

Beck, M. 1981. *Government Spending: Trends and Issues.* New York: Praeger.

_____. 1979. "Public Sector Growth: Real Perspective." *Public Finance*, 36 (3): 313–56.

_____. 1976. "The Expanding Public Sector: Some Contrary Evidence." *National Tax Journal*, 57 (March): 415–26.

Bennett, J. T., and M. H. Johnson. 1983. *The Political Economy of Federal Growth: 1959–1978*. College Station, Texas: Center for Education and Research in Free Enterprise.

Bennett, J. T., and W. P. Orzechowski. 1983. "The Voting Behavior of Bureaucrats." *Public Choice*, 41 (2): 271–84.

Berman, L. 1979. *The Office of Management and Budget and the Presidency, 1921–1979*. Princeton, N.J.: Princeton University Press.

Berry, W. D. 1984. *Nonrecursive Causal Models*. Beverly Hills, Calif.: Sage.

Berry, W. D., and D. Lowery. 1984a. "The Measurement of Government Size: Implications for the Study of Government Growth." *Journal of Politics*, 46 (November): 1193–206.

_____. 1984b. "The Growing Cost of Government: A Test of Two Explanations." *Social Science Quarterly*, 65 (September): 735–49.

Berry, W. D., and L. Sigelman. 1981. "Communication." *American Political Science Review*, 75 (September): 728–30.

Bingham, R. D., B. W. Hawkins, and F. T. Hebert. 1978. *The Politics of Raising State and Local Revenue*. New York: Praeger.

Bird, R. M. 1971. "Wagner's 'Law' of Expanding State Activity." *Public Finance/Finances Publiques*, 26 (March): 1–26.

Boaz, D. 1982. "The Reagan Budget: The Deficit That Didn't Have to Be." Cato Policy Analysis Paper, Washington, D.C.: The Cato Institute.

Borcherding, E. 1977a. *Budgets and Bureaucrats*. Durham, N.C.: Duke University Press.

_____. 1977b. "One Hundred Years of Public Spending, 1870–1970." In *Budgets and Bureaucrats*, edited by T. E. Borcherding, pp. 19–44. Durham, N.C.: Duke University Press.

_____. 1977c. "The Sources of Growth of Public Expenditures in the United States, 1902–1970." In *Budgets and Bureaucrats*, edited by T. E. Borcherding, pp. 45–70. Durham, N.C.: Duke University Press.

Boskin, M. J. 1982. "Assessing the Appropriate Role of Government in the Economy." In *The Federal Budget: Economics and Politics*, edited by M. J. Boskin and A. Wildavsky, pp. 63–88. San Francisco: Institute for Contemporary Studies.

Bradford, M. A., R. A. Malt, and E. Oates. 1969. "The Rising Cost of Local Public Services." *National Tax Journal*, 22 (June): 185–202.

Break, G. 1982. "Government Spending Trends in the Postwar Era." In *The Federal Budget: Economics and Politics*, edited by M. J. Boskin and A. Wildavsky, pp. 39–62. San Francisco: Institute for Contemporary Studies.

Brennan, G., and J. Pincus. 1983. "The Growth of Government: Do the Figures Tell Us What We Want to Know?" In *Why Governments Grow: Measuring Public Sector Size*, edited by C. L. Taylor. Beverly Hills, Calif.: Sage.

Brenton, A., and R. Wintrobe. 1982. *The Logic of Bureaucratic Conduct*. Cambridge: Cambridge University Press.

Brunner, R. D., and K. Leipelt. 1972. "Data Analysis, Process Analysis and System Change." *Midwest Journal of Political Science*, 16 (November): 538–69.

Buchanan, J. M. 1977. "Why Does Government Grow?" in *Budgets and Bureaucrats*, edited by T. E. Borcherding, pp. 3–18, Durham, N.C.: Duke University Press.

_____. 1975. *The Limits of Liberty: Between Anarchy and the Leviathan*. Chicago: The University of Chicago Press.

_____.1954. "Individual Choice in Voting and the Market." *Journal of Political Economy*, 62 (August).

Buchanan, J. M., and G. Tullock. 1977. "The Expanding Public Sector: Wagner Squared." *Public Choice*, 31 (Fall): 147–50.

Buchanan, J. M., and R. E. Wagner. 1978. *Fiscal Responsibility in Constitutional Democracy*. Leiden: Martinus Nijhoff.

_____. 1977. *Democracy in Deficit: The Political Legacy of Lord Keynes*. New York: Academic Press.

Burkhead, J., and J. Miner. 1971. *Public Expenditure*. Chicago: Adline.

Bush, W. C., and A. T. Denzau. 1977. "The Voting Behavior of Bureaucrats and Public Sector Growth." In *Budgets and Bureaucrats*, edited by T. E. Borcherding, pp. 90–99. Durham, N.C.: Duke University Press.

Cameron, D. 1978. "The Expansion of the Public Economy: A Comparative Analysis." *American Political Science Review*, 72 (December): 1243–61.

Caputo, D. 1975. "New Perspectives on the Public Policy Implications of Defense and Welfare Expenditures." *Policy Science*, 6 (4): 423–46.

Caspary, W. 1967. "Richardson's Model of Arms Races: Description, Critique, and an Alternative Model." *International Studies Quarterly*, 11 (2): 63–88.

Citrin, J. 1979. "Do People Want Something for Nothing?: Public Opinion on Taxes and Spending." *National Tax Journal*, 32 (June): 113–29.

Courant, P. N., E. M. Gramlich, and D. L. Rubinfeld. 1980. "Why Voters Support Tax Limitation Amendments: The Michigan Case." *National Tax Journal*, 33 (March): 1–20.

_____. 1979. "Tax Limitation and the Demand for Public Services in Michigan." *National Tax Journal*, 32 (June): 147–58.

Cowart, A. T. 1978. "The Economic Policies of European Governments, Part II." *British Journal of Political Science*, 8 (October): 425–39.

Craig, D., and A. J. Heins. 1980. "The Effect of Tax Elasticity on Government Spending." *Public Choice*, 35 (3): 267–75.

Dahl, R. A. 1961. *Who Governs?* New Haven, Conn.: Yale University Press.

Davis, O., M. H. A. Dempster, and A. Wildavsky. 1966. "A Theory of the Budgetary Process." *American Political Science Review*, 60 (September): 529–47.

_____. 1974. "Toward a Predictive Theory of Government Expenditure: U. S. Domestic Appropriations." *British Journal of Political Science*, 4 (October): 419–52.

Dawson, R. E., and J. Robinson. 1963. "Interparty Competition, Economic Variables, and Welfare Policies in the American States." *Journal of Politics*, 25 (May): 264–89.

DeBartola, G., and P. Fortune. 1982. "The Demand for Public Service: Inferences from Municipal Bond Referenda." *National Tax Journal*, 35 (1): 55–68.

Dempster, M. H. A., and A. Wildavsky. 1973. "On Change: Or There Is No Magic Size for an Increment." *Political Studies*, 27 (2): 55–68.

Department of Defense. 1984. *Military Manpower Statistics*. Washington, D.C.: United States Department of Defense.

Deutsch, K. W. 1983. "The Public Sector: Some Concepts and Indicators." In *Why Governments Grow: Measuring Public Sector Size*, edited by C. L. Taylor, pp. 25–32. Beverly Hills, Calif.: Sage.

Diba, B. T. 1982. "A Note on 'Public Sector Growth: A Real Perspective.'" *Public Finance*, 37 (1): 114–19.

Domke, W. K., R. C. Eichenberg, and C. M. Kelleher. 1983. "The Illusion of Choice: Defense and Welfare in Advanced Industrial Nations." *American Political Science Review*, 77 (March): 19–35.

Downs, A. 1980. "Would a Constitutional Amendment Limit Regulation and Inflation?" In *The Constitution and the Budget*, edited by W. S. Moore and R. G. Penner, pp. 95–100. Washington, D.C.: American Enterprise Institute.

_____. 1966. *Inside Bureaucracy*. Boston: Little, Brown.

_____. 1960. "Why the Government Budget Is Too Small in a Democracy." *World Politics*, 12: 541–63.

_____. 1957. *An Economic Theory of Democracy*. New York: Harper and Row.

Dubin, E. 1977. "The Expanding Public Sector: Some Contrary Evidence — A Comment." *National Tax Journal*, 30 (1): 95.

Due, J. F., and A. F. Friedlander. 1977. *Government Finance*. Homewood, Ill.: R. D. Irwin.

Dye, T. 1966. *Politics, Economics, and the Public: Policy Outcomes in the American States*. Chicago: Rand McNally.

Enrick, N. 1964. "A Further Study of Income Tax Consciousness." *National Tax Journal*, 17 (September): 169–73.

Fabricant, S. 1952. *The Trend of Government Activity in the United States since 1900*. New York: National Bureau of Economic Research.

Fenno, R. 1966. *Power of the Purse*. Boston: Little, Brown.

Fiorina, M. P. 1984. "Flagellating the Federal Bureaucracy." In *The Political Economy*, edited by T. Ferguson and J. Rogers, pp. 224–34. Armonk, N.Y.: M. E. Sharpe.

_____. 1977. *Congress: Keystone of the Washington Establishment*. New Haven, Conn.: Yale University Press.

Fisher, G. 1964. "Interstate Variation in State and Local Government Expenditure." *National Tax Journal*, 17 (March): 57–74.

Fisher, L. 1975. *Presidential Spending Power*. Princeton, N.J.: Princeton University Press..

Formuzis, P., and A. Puri. 1980. "Inflation, Progressivity, and the State Income Tax." In *Taxing and Spending Policy,* edited by W. Samuels and L. Wade. Lexington, Mass.: Lexington Books.

Frey, B. S., and F. Schneider. 1978., "An Empirical Study of Politico-Economic Interaction in the United States." *Review of Economics and Statistics,* 60 (May): 174–83.

Friedman, M. 1978. *Tax Limitation, Inflation and the Role of Government*. Dallas, Texas: The Fisher Institute.

_____. 1962. *Capitalism and Freedom*. Chicago: The University of Chicago Press.

Friedman, M., and R. Friedman. 1980. *Free to Choose*. New York: Harcourt, Brace, and Jovanovich.

Fry, B. R., and R. F. Winters. 1970. "The Politics of Redistribution." *American Journal of Political Science,* 64 (June): 388–94.

Galbraith, J. K. 1969. *The New Industrial State*. New York: Pelican Books.

_____. 1958. *The Affluent Society*. Boston: Houghton Mifflin.

Gilder, G. 1981. *Wealth and Poverty*. Toronto: Bantam Books.

Goetz, C. J. 1977. "Fiscal Illusion in State and Local Finance." In *Budgets and Bureaucrats,* edited by T. E. Borcherding, pp. 176–87. Durham, N.C.: Duke University Press.

Goodsell, C. T. 1983. *The Case for Bureaucracy*. Chatham, N.J.: Chatham Books.

Gould, F. 1983. "The Growth of Public Expenditures: Theory and Evidence from Six Advanced Democracies." In *Why Governments Grow: Measuring Public Sector Size,* edited by C. L. Taylor, pp. 217–39. Beverly Hills, Calif: Sage.

Gramlich, E. M., and D. L. Rubinfeld. 1982. "Voting on Public Spending: Differences between Public Employees, Transfer Recipients, and Private Workers." *Journal of Policy Analysis and Management,* 1 (4): 516–33.

Gray, V. 1976. "Models of Comparative State Politics: A Comparison of Cross-Sectional and Time-Series Analysis." *American Journal of Political Science,* 20 (May): 235–56.

Grodzins, M. 1960. "American Political Parties and the American System." *Western Political Quarterly*, 13 (December): 974–98.

Gupta, S. P. 1968. "Public Expenditures and Economic Development — A Cross-Section Analysis." *Finanzarchir*, (October), pp. 26–41.

Haider, D. 1974. *When Governments Come to Washington*. New York: The Free Press.

Hansen, S. B. 1983. *The Politics of Taxation: Revenue without Representation*. New York: Praeger.

Hansen, S. B., and P. Cooper. 1980. "State Revenue Elasticity and Expenditure Growth." In *Taxing and Spending Policy*, edited by W. Samuels and L. Wade, pp. 35–42. Lexington, Mass.: Lexington Books.

Harrison, B., and S. Kanter. 1980. "The Political Economy of States' Job-Creation Incentives." In *State and Local Tax Revolt: New Directions for the 80s*, edited by D. Tipps and L. Webb, pp. 277–88. Washington, D.C.: Conference on Alternative State and Local Policies.

Hartman, R. W. 1982. "Federal Employee Compensation and the Budget." In *The Federal Budget: Economics and Politics*, edited by M. J. Boskin and A. Wildavsky, pp. 263–80. San Francisco: Institute for Contemporary Studies.

Heidenheimer, A. J. 1975. *Comparative Public Policy*. New York: St. Martin's Press.

Heller, P. S. 1981. "Diverging Trends in the Shares of Nominal and Real Government Expenditures in GDP: Implications for Policy." *National Tax Journal*, 34 (1): 61–74.

Hibbs, D. A. 1974. "Problems in Statistical Estimation and Causal Inference in Dynamic Time-Series Models." In *Sociological Methodology*, edited by H. Costner, pp. 252–308. San Francisco: Jossey Bass.

Hibbs, D. A., and H. J. Madsen. 1981. "Public Reactions to the Growth of Taxation and Government Expenditure." *World Politics*, 33 (3): 413–35.

Hofferbert, R. I. 1981. "Communication." *American Political Science Review*, 75 (September): 722–25.

Huntington, S. 1961. "Interservice Competition and the Political Roles of the Armed Services." *American Political Science Review*, 55 (March): 40–52.

Ippolito, D. S. 1981. *Congressional Spending Power*. Ithaca, N.Y.: Cornell University Press.

Jacobe, D. J. 1977. "Federal Propensities to Tax and Spend." In *Budgets and*

Bureaucrats, edited by T. E. Borcherding, pp. 169–75. Durham, N.C.: Duke University Press.

Jarvis, H. 1979. *I'm Mad As Hell.* New York: Times Books.

Jennings, E. T. 1980. "Urban Riots and the Growth of State Welfare Expenditures." In *Taxing and Spending Policy,* edited by W. Samuels and L. Wade, pp. 43–50. Lexington, Mass.: Lexington Books.

_____. 1979. "Competition, Constituencies, and Welfare Policies in American States." *American Political Science Review,* 73 (December): 414–29.

Jewell, M., and D. Olson. 1978. *American State Political Parties and Elections.* Homewood, Ill.: Dorsey Press.

Jones, E. T. 1974. "Political Change and Spending Shifts in the American States." *American Politics Quarterly,* 2 (2): 159–78.

Kamlet, M. S., and D. C. Mowery. 1983. "Budgetary Side Payments and Government Growth." *American Journal of Political Science,* 27 (November): 636–64.

_____. 1980. "The Budgetary Base in Federal Resource Allocation." *American Journal of Political Science,* 24 (November): 804–21.

Kanter, A. 1972. "Congress and the Defense Budget: 1960–1970." *American Political Science Review,* 66 (March): 129–43.

Katz, C. J., V. A. Mahler, and M. G. Franz. 1983. "The Impact of Taxes on Growth and Distribution in Developed Capitalist Countries: A Cross-National Study." *American Political Science Review,* 77 (December): 871–86.

Kau, J. B., and P. H. Rubin. 1981. "The Size of Government." *Public Choice,* 37: 261–74.

_____. 1979. "Self-Interest, Ideology, and Logrolling in Congressional Elections." *Journal of Law and Economics,* 22 (October): 365–84.

Kaufman, H. 1976. *Red Tape.* Washington, D.C.: The Brookings Institution.

Keech, W. R. 1980. "Elections and Macroeconomic Policy Optimization." *American Journal of Political Science,* 24 (May): 345–67.

Kelly, A. C. 1976. "Demographic Change and the Size of the Government Sector." *Southern Economic Journal,* 43 (4): 1056–66.

Key, V. O. 1949. *Southern Politics.* New York: Alfred A. Knopf.

Kiewiet, R. D., and M. D. McCubbins. 1985. "Congressional Appropriations and the Electoral Connection." *Journal of Politics,* 47 (February): 59–82.

Krasner, S. D. 1976. "State Power and the Structure of International Trade." *World Politics,* 28: 317–47.

Larkey, P. D., C. Stolp, and M. Winer. 1984. "Why Does Government Grow?" In *Public Sector Performance,* edited by T. C. Miller, pp. 65–101. Baltimore, Md.: The Johns Hopkins University Press.

_____. 1981. "Theorizing about the Growth of Government: A Research Assessment." *Journal of Public Policy,* 1: 157–220.

Lekachman, R. 1982. *Greed Is Not Enough: Reaganomics.* New York: Pantheon.

Lembruch, F. 1977. "Liberal Corporatism and Party Government." *Comparative Political Studies,* 10 (1): 91–126.

Lerner, A. P. 1978. "Keynesianism: Alive, If Not So Well, at Forty." In *Fiscal Responsibility in Constitutional Democracy,* edited by J. M. Buchanan and R. E. Wagner, pp. 59–69. Boston: Martinus Nijhoff.

Lewis–Beck, M., and T. Rice. 1984. "Government Growth in the United States." *Journal of Politics,* 47 (February): 2–30.

Lindbeck, A. 1976. "Stabilization Policy in Open Economies with Endogenous Politicians." *American Economic Review,* 66: 1-19.

Lindsay, C. M., and D. Norman. 1977. "Reopening the Question of Government Spending." In *Budgets and Bureaucrats,* edited by T. E. Borcherding. Durham, N.C.: Duke University Press.

Lowery, D. 1985. "Political Incentives and Revenue Structures in the American States: A Test of the Fiscal Illusion Hypothesis." Paper presented at the Southwest Social Science Association meeting, Houston, Texas, March.

_____. 1983a. "The Hidden Impact of Fiscal Caps: Implications of the Beck Phenomenon." *Public Budgeting and Finance,* 3 (Autumn): 19–32.

_____. 1983b. "Limitations on Taxing and Spending Powers: An Assessment of Their Effectiveness." *Social Science Quarterly,* 63 (June): 247–63.

Lowery, D., and W. D. Berry. 1983. "The Growth of Government in the United States: An Empirical Assessment of Competing Explanations." *American Journal of Political Science,* 27 (November): 665–94.

Lowery, D., and L. Sigelman. 1982. "Party Identification and Public Spending Priorities in the American Electorate." *Political Studies*, 30: 221–35.

McGuire, T. G. 1981. "Budget Maximizing Government Agencies: An Empirical Test." *Public Choice*, 36: 313–22.

McIntyre, R., and D. Tipps. 1983. *Inequality and Decline: How the Reagan Policies Are Affecting the American Taxpayer and Economy*. Washington, D.C.: Center on Budget and Policy Priorities.

McKenzie, R. B., and R. J. Staff. 1978. "Revenue Sharing and Monopoly Government." *Public Choice*, 33 (3): 93–98.

Mann, A. J. 1980. "Wagner's Law: An Econometric Test for Mexico, 1925–1976." *National Tax Journal*, 33 (June): 189–201.

Margolis, J. 1981. "Comments on Aranson and Ordeshook Paper." In *Tax and Expenditure Limitations*, edited by H. F. Ladd and T. N. Nicholson, pp. 177–90. Washington, D.C.: The Urban Institute.

Mariotti, S. 1978. "An Economic Analysis of the Voting on Michigan's Tax and Expenditure Limitation Amendment." *Public Choice*, 33 (Fall): 15–26.

Marquette, J., and K. Hinkley. 1981. "Competition, Control, and Spurious Covariation: A Longitudinal Analysis of State Spending." *American Journal of Political Science*, 25 (May): 362–75.

Meier, K. J. 1975. "Representative Bureaucracy: An Empirical Analysis." *American Political Science Review*, 69 (June): 526–42.

Meltsner, A. 1982. "Budget Control through Political Action." In *The Federal Budget: Economics and Politics*, edited by M. J. Boskin and A. Wildavsky, pp. 315–32. San Francisco: Institute for Contemporary Studies.

_____. 1971. *The Politics of City Revenue*. Berkeley, Calif.: University of California Press.

Mikesell, J. 1978. "Election Periods and State Policy Cycles." *Public Choice*, 20: 49–58.

Miller, G., and T. M. Moe. 1983. "Bureaucrats, Legislators, and the Size of Government." *American Political Science Review*, 77 (June): 297–322.

Mueller, D. 1979. *Public Choice*. Cambridge: Cambridge University Press.

Muller, T. 1984. "A Demographic Perspective." In *Public Sector Performance*, edited by T. C. Miller, pp. 131–60. Baltimore, Md.: The Johns Hopkins University Press.

Musgrave, R. A. 1981. "Leviathan Cometh — or Does He?" In *Tax and Expenditure Limitations*, edited by H. Ladd and T. N. Tideman, pp. 77–120. Washington, D.C.: The Urban Institute.

____.1969. *Fiscal Systems*. New Haven, Conn.: Yale University Press.

Musgrave, R. A., and Culberton, J. M. 1953. "The Growth of Public Expenditures in the United States, 1890–1948." *National Tax Journal*, 6 (2): 97–115.

Nathan, R. P. 1983. *The Administrative Presidency*. New York: John Wiley.

Niemi, R. G., and H. F. Weisberg. 1976. *Controversies in American Voting Behavior*. San Francisco: W. H. Freeman.

Niskanen, W. A. 1978. "The Prospect for a Liberal Democracy." In *Fiscal Responsibility in Constitutional Democracy*, edited by J. M. Buchanan and R. E. Wagner, pp. 157–73. Leden: Martinus Nijhoff.

____. 1971. *Bureaucracy and Representative Government*. Chicago: Aldine and Atherton.

Nutter, G. W. 1978. *Growth of Government in the West*. Washington, D.C.: American Enterprise Institute.

O'Connor, J. 1973. *The Fiscal Crisis of the State*. New York: St. Martin's Press.

Olson, M. 1982. *The Rise and Decline of Nations*. New Haven, Conn.: Yale University Press.

____. 1980. "Is the Balanced Budget Amendment Another Form of Prohibition?" In *The Constitution and the Budget*, edited by W. S. Moore and R. G. Penner, pp. 91–94. Washington, D.C.: American Enterprise Institute.

____. 1965. *The Logic of Collective Action*. Cambridge, Mass.: Harvard University Press.

Orzechowski, W. 1977. "Economic Models of Bureaucracy: Survey, Extensions, and Evidence." In *Budgets and Bureaucrats*, edited by T. E. Borcherding, pp. 229–59. Durham, N.C.: Duke University Press.

____. 1974. "Labor Intensity, Productivity, and the Growth of the Federal Sector." *Public Choice*, 19: 123–6.

Ostrom, C. W., Jr. 1978. "A Reactive Linkage Model of the U.S. Defense Expenditure Policy-Process." *American Political Science Review,* 72 (September): 941–57.

Ostrom, C. W., Jr., and R. Marra. 1986. "U.S. Defense Spending and the Soviet Estimate." *American Political Science Review,* 80 (September): 819–42.

Ott, A. 1980. "Has the Growth of Government in the West Been Halted?" In *Taxing and Spending Policy,* edited by W. Samuels and L. Wade, pp. 3–16. Lexington, Mass.: Lexington Books.

Ott, D. J., and Ott, A. F. 1969. *Federal Budget Policy.* Washington, D.C.: The Brookings Institution.

Page, B. I. 1983. *Who Gets What from Government?* Berkeley, Calif. University of California Press.

Palmer, J. L., and I. V. Sawhill. 1984. *The Reagan Record.* Washington, D.C.: The Urban Institute.

____. 1982. *The Reagan Experiment.* Washington, D.C.: The Urban Institute.

Peacock, A. R., and J. Wiseman. 1961. *The Growth of Public Expenditure in the United Kingdom.* Princeton, N.J.: Princeton University Press.

Peltzman, S. 1980. "The Growth of Government." *Journal of Law and Economics,* 23 (2): 209–87.

Peters, B. G. 1980. "Public Employment in the United States: Growth and Change." Working paper, Center for the Study of Public Policy, Glasgow: University of Strathclyde.

Pigou, A. C. 1946. *The Economics of Welfare,* 4th ed. London: McMillan.

Pjerrou-Desrouches, L. 1981. "Fiscal Role and Partisanship in California's Budgetary Process." *Public Budgeting and Finance,* 1 (Fall): 3–15.

Plaut, T., and J. Pluta. 1983. "Business Climate, Taxes and Expenditures, and State Industrial Growth in the United States." *Southern Economic Journal,* 50 (July): 99–119.

Plotnick, R. D., and R. F. Winters. 1986. "Political Liberalism, Party Control, and Redistribution in the American States." Paper presented to the Midwest Political Science Association, Chicago, April.

Polsby, N. 1963. *Community Power and Political Theory.* New Haven, Conn.: Yale University Press.

Pommerehne, W. W., and F. Schneider. 1978. "Fiscal Illusion, Political Institutions, and Local Public Spending." *Kyklos,* 31 (3): 381–407.

Rabushka, A. 1982. "Fiscal Responsibility: Will Anything Less Than a Constitutional Amendment Do?" In *The Federal Budget: Economics and Politics,* edited by M. J. Boskin and A. Wildavsky, pp. 333–45. San Francisco: Institute for Contemporary Studies.

Rabushka, A., and P. Ryan. 1982. *The Tax Revolt.* Stanford, Calif. The Hoover Institute.

Reagan, M., and J. Sanzone. 1981. *The New Federalism.* New York: Oxford University Press.

Richardson, L. F. 1960. *Arms and Insecurity: A Mathematical Study of the Causes and Origins of War.* Pittsburgh, Pa.: Boxwood.

Riker, W. H. 1980. "Constitutional Limits as Self-Denying Ordinances." In *The Constitution and the Budget,* edited by W. S. Moore and R. G. Penner. Washington, D.C.: American Enterprise Institute.

Rose, R. 1984. *Understanding Big Government: The Programme Approach.* London: Sage.

_____. 1983. "Disaggregating the Concept of Government." In *Why Governments Grow: Measuring the Size of Government,* edited by C. L. Taylor, pp. 157–76. Beverly Hills, Calif.

_____. 1980. "Changes in Public Employment: A Multidimensional Comparative Analysis." Studies in Public Policy 61, Glasgow: University of Strathclyde.

Rousseas, S. 1982. *The Political Economy of Reaganomics: A Critique.* Armonk, N.Y.: M. E. Sharpe.

Rundquist, B. S. 1980. *Political Benefits.* Lexington, Mass.: Lexington Books.

Russett, B. M. 1969. *What Price Vigilance?* New Haven, Conn.: Yale University Press.

Samuels, W. 1976. "Ideology in Economics." Mimeo, East Lansing, Mich. Department of Economics, Michigan State University.

Samuels, W., and J. M. Buchanan. 1975. "On Some Fundamental Issues in Political Economy: An Exchange of Correspondence." *Journal of Economic Issues,* 9

(March): 15–38.

Savas, E. S. 1982. *Privatizing the Public Sector*. Chatham, N.J.: Chatham House.

Schmid, A. A. 1978. *Property, Power, and Public Choice*. New York: Praeger.

Schumpeter, J. 1950. *Capitalism, Socialism, and Democracy*. New York: Harper and Row.

Shannon, J. 1981. "The Politics of Fiscal Containment: Effects on State and Local Government and the Federal Aid System." In *Perspectives on Taxing and Spending Limitations in the United States*, edited by C. B. Tyer and M. W. Taylor. Columbia, S.C.: Bureau of Governmental Research and Service, University of South Carolina.

Sharkansky, I. 1967. "Government Expenditures and Public Services in the American States." *American Political Science Review*, 20 (December): 1066–77.

Sigelman, L. 1986. "The Bureaucrat as Budget Maximizer." *Public Budgeting and Finance*, 6 (1): 50–59.

Spann, R. M. 1977a. "Public Versus Private Provision of Governmental Service." In *Budgets and Bureaucrats*, edited by T. E. Borcherding, pp. 100–29. Durham, N.C.: Duke University Press.

_____.1977b. "The Macroeconomics of Unbalanced Growth and the Expanding Public Sector." *Journal of Public Economics*, 8: 397–404.

Stein, H. 1978. "The Decline of the Balanced Budget Doctrine or How the Good Guys Finally Lost." In *Fiscal Responsibility in Constitutional Democracy*, edited by J. M. Buchanan and R. E. Wagner, pp. 35–52. Boston: Martinus Nijhoff.

Stigler, G. 1982. *The Economist as Preacher*. Chicago: University of Chicago Press.

Sundquist, J. L. 1969. *Making Federalism Work*. Washington, D.C.: The Brookings Institution.

Tarschys, D. 1975. "The Growth of Public Expenditures: Nine Models of Explanation." *Scandinavian Political Studies*, 10: 9–31.

Taylor, C. L. 1983. *Why Governments Grow: Measuring Public Sector Size*. Beverly Hills, Calif.: Sage.

Thurow, L. C. 1980. *The Zero-Sum Society: Distribution and the Possibilities for Change*. New York: Basic Books.

Tiegen, R. L. 1980. "Trends and Cycles in the Composition of the Federal Budget." In

Taxing and Spending Policy, edited by W. Samuels and L. Wade. Lexington, Mass.: Lexington Books.

Tufte, E. R. 1978. *Political Control of the Economy*. Princeton, N.J.: Princeton University Press.

Tullock, G. 1977. "What Is to Be Done?" In *Budgets and Bureaucrats: The Sources of Government Growth*, edited by T. E. Borcherding, pp. 275–88. Durham, N.C.: Duke University Press.

_____. 1965. *The Politics of Bureaucracy*. Washington, D.C.: Public Affairs Press.

Tullock, G., and J. M. Buchanan. 1977. "The Expanding Public Sector: Wagner Squared." *Public Choice*, 31 (Fall): 147–50.

Vickrey, W. 1961. "The Burden of the Public Debt: A Comment." *American Economic Review*, 51 (March): 132–7.

Wagner, A. 1877. *Finanzwissenschaft*, Part 1. Leipzig: C. F. Winter.

Wagner, R. E. 1976. "Revenue Structure, Fiscal Illusion, and the Budgetary Choice." *Public Choice*, 25: 45–61.

Wagner, R. E., R. D. Tollison, A. Rabushka, and J. T. Noonan. 1982. *Balanced Budgets, Fiscal Responsibility, and the Constitution*. Washington, D.C.: Cato Institute.

Wagstaff, J. V. 1965. "Income Tax Consciousness under Withholding." *Southern Economics Journal*, 32 (July): 73–80.

Wanat, J. 1978. *Introduction to Budgeting*. North Scituate, Mass.: Duxbury Press.

Wanniski, J. 1979. *The Way the World Works*. New York: Simon and Schuster.

Ward, M. D. 1984. "Differential Paths to Parity: A Study of the Contemporary Arms Race." *American Political Science Review*, 78 (June): 297–317.

Whiteley, P. F. 1983. "The Political Economy of Economic Growth." *European Journal of Political Research*, 11 (1): 3–18.

Wildavsky, A. 1980. *How to Limit Government Spending*. Berkeley, Calif.: University of California Press.

_____. 1975. *Budgeting: A Comparative Theory of the Budgetary Process*. Boston: Little, Brown.

_____. 1964. *The Politics of the Budgetary Process.* Boston: Little, Brown.

Wilensky, H. L. 1978. *The Welfare State and Equality.* Berkeley: Calif.: University of California Press.

Wilson, J. Q. 1975. "The Rise of the Bureaucratic State." *The Public Interest,* 41 (Fall): 77–103.

Winters, R. F. 1976. "Party Control and Policy Change." *American Journal of Political Science,* 20 (November): 597–636.

Witte, J. 1982. "Incremental Theory and Income Tax Policy: The Problem of Too Much, Not Too Little Change." Paper presented at the American Political Science Association meetings, Denver, Colorado, September.

Yates, D. 1982. *Bureaucratic Democracy.* Cambridge, Mass.: Harvard University Press.

INDEX

ABOUT THE AUTHORS

William D. Berry received his Ph.D. at the University of Minnesota in 1980 and is currently Associate Professor of Political Science at the University of Kentucky. His areas of specialization are public policy, political economy, and research methodology. He has recently been involved in studies of government regulation, public sector growth, and budgeting. Professor Berry has published numerous papers in scholarly journals such as *Journal of Politics* and *American Journal of Political Science* and is on the editorial board of the latter. He is also author of *Multiple Regression in Practice, Nonrecursive Causal Models,* and coeditor of *New Tools for Social Scientists: Applications and Advances in Research Methods.*

David Lowery received his Ph.D. at Michigan State University in 1981 and is currently Associate Professor of Political Science at the University of North Carolina at Chapel Hill. He has also served as policy analyst with the Michigan Department of Treasury and was chief legislative aide to the Committee on Taxation of the Michigan House of Representatives. His primary work has been on the politics of public finance and administrative politics. Professor Lowery has published numerous articles on these topics in such scholarly journals as *American Political Science Review, Journal of Politics, American Journal of Political Science, Western Political Quarterly,* and *Social Science Quarterly.*